The Single-Minded Christian Soldier

Strengthening Strategies that Cannot Be...Left Behind
To Help Ensure Others Are Not...Left Behind

Bruce Peltier

A unique blend of fact, fiction, humor and spirituality

Selah Press PUBLISHING

The Single-Minded Christian Soldier:
Strengthening Strategies that Cannot Be...Left Behind
To Help Ensure Others Are Not...Left Behind

Editor: Loral Robben Pepoon, Cowriterpro
Cover Design: Jennifer Smith, Eco-Office Gals
Printed in the United States of America, Published by Selah Press, LLC

Copyright © 2015 Bruce Peltier

ISBN-13: 978-0692621387 (Selah Press)
ISBN-10: 0692621385

For information on getting permission for reprints and excerpts, visit:
PeltierBooksandMusic.com

Dedication

To my wife:

Her music enriches my life
Her faith keeps me focused
Her dedication encourages me to strive for excellence
Her life…completes mine.

It was through the music ministry of my wife that I learned how to praise God. Her relentless pursuit to please the Father taught me the importance of a disciplined life. Her heart demonstrates the quality that is required to please Him and her dedication instilled in me the need to… *"study to show thy self approved"* (2 Timothy 2:15).

She monitors my silly moments and keeps me focused. She has always given more to our marriage than she has received. She has served selflessly in churches for nearly 50 years.

Of the things I have done well, they are to her credit (the others were mostly accidental).

And, to my mom:

I know where you are now and I try to rejoice with you every day about that. But of course, I miss you.

My mother was married to a military officer who fought in World War II, Korea and Vietnam twice. She raised three boys practically by herself. She was also a pastor's wife and a faithful help-meet.

Mom, you may not have worn a uniform, but you are certainly…a hero and a veteran.

To my earthly father:

It seems that as I sift through papers, sermons and other artifacts of the legacy my father left behind, I am continually reminded of what I have taken for granted for so long.

I find a patriarchal outline of what a man, a soldier, a husband, a minister, father and mentor should be. As his life becomes more clearly defined by these new discoveries and memories revisited, it reveals more than just the details of his accomplishments. More important were his motives and his faith that produced such amazing fruit. All of these qualities combined have become the justification and constant source of my admiration for this man I called, "Dad."

As I reminisce, ponder and celebrate the evidence I rediscover, I am also challenged to follow his path, to strive to duplicate his goals and to do so with the same motives…all by faith. I am challenged to walk in the boots of this soldier. Boots that indeed, walked his talk. What a privilege to be my father's son.

To my Heavenly Father:

To know You and to submit to Your perfect will should be our highest goal. If reading this book brings You any glory, the credit and the praise is Yours alone.

What a privilege to be my Heavenly Father's son.

Introduction

Whether you are a newly converted Christian recruit who is just learning to be a soldier or a senior veteran of the faith, I challenge you to examine yourself regularly using the 36 strengthening strategies presented in this book. If you care about others not being left behind, and if you want them to have the peace you have in this life and to join you in Heaven, pour over the contents of this book.

The strategies and their associated tactics serve both as a new single-minded soldier instruction manual and as a refresher course who completed basic Christian training years ago. These strategies will help you fortify your faith, focus for success on your overall disciple-making mission and clarify your upcoming marching orders with confidence.

Why do these strategies work? Because they help you hear, learn and execute God's plan through obedience to God's instructions in the Bible. This obedience not only includes being properly equipped and committed for God's purposes, but it also brings transformation, fulfillment and peace as you and other single-minded soldiers become more Christ-like in character.

These transformations, in turn, will have ripple effects. When others see and hear about the differences in the lives of single-minded soldiers, they too will want to "enlist." They will want to experience the same supernatural peace and joy exhibited by their comrades—even in the midst of life's battles.

So, get ready to march on, single-minded soldier! Your greatest mission is at hand!

Contents

Background Information   1

1   **How to Read with Your Head, but Think with Your Heart: Part 1**   5

Strengthening Strategy: Discovering where salvation is actually decided.

2   **How to Read with Your Head, but Think with Your Heart: Part 2**   13

Strengthening Strategy: Understanding what you are saved "from" and saved "to"—conditional and unconditional covenants.

3   **Prayer, Meditation…or Both?**   19

Strengthening Strategy: Using spiritual eyes, spiritual ears and more.

4   **The Dangers of Juicing**   23

Strengthening Strategy: Maintaining the purity of the Gospel message.

5   **Grace Du Jour**   27

Strengthening Strategy: Receiving the offer of introductory grace: pure and simple, but accurate.

6   **Grace Realized**   31

Strengthening Strategy: Appropriating Saving Grace…two sides of the same coin?

7   **Ignorance Is Not Bliss**   35

Strengthening Strategy: Delaying the inevitable casts shadows on the truth.

8   **The "KISS" Principle**   39

*Strengthening Strategy: **K**eeping **I**t **S**imple **S**aint—Is it supply and demand or demand to supply?*

9   **The Politically Correct Gospel**   45

Strengthening Strategy: Determining what really needs to be left behind.

10   **Fulfilling the General Order**   49

Strengthening Strategy: Knowing some orders allow for innovation and flexibility; others do not.

11   **Spiritually Blindsided**   57

Strengthening Strategy: Being aware of the potential of friendly fire.

12 **So Butch Says to Sundance…**   63
    *Strengthening Strategy: Identifying and dealing with the relentless
    pursuit of human judgment.*

13 **Rapture or Rupture?**   69
    *Strengthening Strategy: Addressing this highly controversial topic that
    could split a church.*

14 **CSI Evangelism**   73
    *Strengthening Strategy: Examining the evidence in Christians' lives so
    that non-believers know the truth.*

15 **Good Fruit or…Wax?**   77
    *Strengthening Strategy: Discerning between what is real and what is
    counterfeit.*

16 **Go Fish!**   81
    *Strengthening Strategy: Casting your nets where the fish are. How,
    where and when?*

17 **Antiquated Progress**   87
    *Strengthening Strategy: Recognizing a contradiction in terms…or is
    this a sign of the times?*

18 **Let's Make a Deal**   91
    Strengthening Strategy: Engaging in total wealth management.

19 **The Enemy of the Church?**   95
    *Strengthening Strategy: Understanding "contemporary praise and
    worship."*

20 **The Dimensions of God**   101
    *Strengthening Strategy: Enrolling and completing Supernatural
    Discovery 101*

21 **Sticks and Stones and Broken Bones—But His Words** 107
    Will Never Harm Me
    *Strengthening Strategy: Trusting in what God allows…even though we
    may not understand it.*

22 **Back Drop or Jaw Drop**   113
    *Strengthening Strategy: Understanding the consequences of living life on
    your own terms.*

23 **The Bride in Beige: "I'm Not Perfect, But I'm Close."** 117
Strengthening Strategy: Not compromising in purity so that you accurately represent Christ's character.

24 **Love and Marriage** 121
Strengthening Strategy: Fitting together like a horse and carriage. Well...Yes and maybe—or maybe not.

25 **Loving for a Lifetime** 127
Strengthening Strategy: Committing to obey instead of relying on feelings.

26 **A Court-Martial Offense** 131
Strengthening Strategy: Knowing the dangers of micromanaging supernatural inspiration, authority and leadership...a slippery slope.

27 **Hot Dog Accountability** 137
Strengthening Strategy: Being accountable to "a higher authority."

28 **Being a Member at the YMCA Is Not Enough** 143
Strengthening Strategy: Committing to a church.

29 **The Complexity of Simplicity** 149
Strengthening Strategy: Comprehending the accuracy and divine inspiration of the Bible.

30 **The Misconception of Conception: Part 1** 155
Strengthening Strategy: Putting a comma after forgiveness, not a period!

31 **The Misconception of Conception: Part 2** 161
Strengthening Strategy: Living the Christian life in your own wisdom and power...hinders growing up in Christ.

32 **Dysfunctional Units: It's Not My Job** 167
Strengthening Strategy: Understanding the difference between being busy and making progress.

33 **Plum Foolish? Or Plum Good?** 173
Strengthening Strategy: Looking for the quality and quantity that pleases God.

34 **Spiritual Multitasking** 177
Strengthening Strategy: Understanding our problems—we don't know...what we don't know.

35 **PC Terrorism**   183
    Strengthening Strategy: Being authentic, recognizing the truth and defending the faith.

36 **Be All you Are**   187
    Strengthening Strategy: Committing to standing tall, being bulletproof and believing that failure is not an option!

    Poem   189
    Acknowledgments   191
    About the Author   192
    Single-Minded Soldier Photos   194

Background Information

Why I chose the title: Single-Minded Soldier

I chose the important message of "single-mindedness" because, as Christians, we need to be clear about who we are and what our goals are to effectively carry out our God-ordained mission. That assignment, given at the moment of salvation, is to love Christ and grow in His character, witness to others and to engage in lifelong discipleship of other soldiers. At the same time, we must eliminate the negative shadows Christians can cast if they are not clear, focused and confident. Soldiers, if properly trained and obedient exemplify commitment, service and clarity of duty—and they are equipped to perform this important, life-saving mission with success.

The following Scripture inspired the title: *"If any of you lacks wisdom [to guide him through a decision or circumstance], he is to ask of [our benevolent] God, who gives to everyone generously and without rebuke or blame, and it will be given to him. But he must ask [for wisdom] in faith, without doubting [God's willingness to help], for the one who doubts is like a billowing surge of the sea that is blown about and tossed by the wind. For such a person ought not to think or expect that he will receive anything [at all] from the Lord,* **being a double-minded man, unstable and restless in all his ways** *[in everything he thinks, feels, or decides]"* (James 1:5–8 Amplified Bible, Classic Edition, AMP).

The opposite of the double-minded man described in this verse is a "single-minded" one. A Christian's single-minded focus can only come as a result of discipleship, knowledge and focus as a result of spiritual enlightenment, discernment and empowerment. The battle comes because this process can be overwhelming for new Christians to grasp right away. The foxholes of a long battle can also be a difficult place for older Christians to remain entrenched.

What prompted me to write.

I was deeply moved with compassion after I read LaHaye's and Jenkin's *Left Behind* series. The books depict end-times problems and the mass chaos faced on Earth by those left behind after millions of people instantly disappear because of the Rapture. The books had a profound effect on me because my experience as a Christian, teacher and pastor for decades taught me that these fictional books were grounded in Scriptural truth—especially the part about unbelievers being left behind.

A simple examination of world events, or observing "the signs of the times" in light of biblical prophecy, could indicate that the Rapture—the theological event that describes the Christians instantly leaving Earth—is approaching at lightning speed.

Therefore, since none of us knows the hour of His return—and because I don't want anyone to be left behind—there is no time like the present to get this information in the hands of Christians in the battle.

My mission, motivation and drive.

My mission is to "rally the troops" or challenge my brothers and sisters in Christ to "step up" their efforts as the battle heats up and the Enemy seems to be taking our territory.

In addition to the nudging of the Holy Spirit, my military background makes the severity and reality of leaving others behind all too real. A soldier prepares, executes and fights to make certain he does not leave anyone on the battlefield. Similarly, we are all in the race and battle of life on earth together.

The good news is that this war has already been won! Jesus won it on the cross and rose from the grave. Those who know Him will celebrate that victory for eternity and will never be left out!

My style and dilemma.

My entire Christian life, I have struggled with the balance to maintain reverence and humility when I enjoy being funny, quick-witted and sometimes a bit sarcastic.

As I considered the content of this book, I decided not to suppress these seemingly opposing attributes—even though using any combination of them is like juggling Jell-O.

I want my worship to be accurate and totally acceptable to the Father and to live a life that demonstrates my faith in everything. I believe I have an average level of intellect, some Bible knowledge and plenty of "church experience." I also believe I have a side that is quick-witted and I try to intermingle it with spirituality. Hopefully the mix works in this book.

I also want my military background, business experiences, Christian training, teaching, preaching and pastoring of almost 50 years to express some interesting perspectives about the Christian life in an interesting, enlightening manner.

My prayer for the book.

I pray that this book will help clarify important principles of living the Christian life so that Christians will be better equipped to live out the disciple-making mission God has called us all to. I pray that everyone we come in contact with will be correctly introduced to the greatest offer anyone could every want or need—the gift of eternal life and the gift of living a fulfilling Christian life today—not just in the sweet by-and-by.

1.

How to Read with Your Head, but Think with Your Heart: Part 1

Strengthening Strategy:
Discovering where salvation is actually decided.

An ancient quote says: *"The journey of a thousand miles begins with the first step."*

So what's the first step to becoming a fully-inducted single-minded Christian soldier? The answer is to decide where to begin.

And, I believe it makes perfect sense to begin at the very beginning of everything. The first four words of the Bible are: *"In the beginning, God..."* (Genesis 1:1, King James Version, hereafter KJV).

If you do not believe these four words—or if you are not willing to learn more about this truth, there is no reason to read the rest of the Bible. It is about God, the Creator of the Universe. If you don't believe those four words, there won't be much for you in this book, either.

But assuming you believe those four words, the next foundational statements that will guide the entire discussion of this book are: *The Bible is a holy book without error and is as applicable today as it was when it was written. It is a book of love and redemption, and it is a blueprint for life on Earth and life throughout eternity.*

As we read the Bible with our minds and internalize the truth found in its pages, we develop a heart of love and gratitude, obedience, worship, praise and honesty that fuel us to learn about or to refresh our knowledge of God. We commit or recommit to run the race, keep the faith and finish the fight.

Another overarching scripture to help us get a bird's eye view of where we are going on our journey of becoming an effective single-minded Christian soldier is: *Ask and keep on asking and it shall be given you; seek and keep on seeking and you shall find; knock and keep on knocking and the door shall be opened to you.* (Luke 11:9, Amplified Classic Version, hereafter AMPC).

Therefore, as we train for our journey as single-minded soldiers, we will transition from asking for intellectual understanding to receiving it, and from receiving to expecting the opening the gates of Heaven to help us make a full commitment to the perfect will of God in our lives.

But, before the floodgates of Heaven open to us, we need to make sure we understand a bit more about the reading with our mind and learning with our heart concept, so let's look at that part in more detail.

As single-minded Christian soldiers, we have to be well trained to learn how to process information correctly in our minds, but then we must go deeper. We must internalize the concepts, rely on the accuracy of training, demonstrate a high level of discipline and exercise sound judgment.

We must also understand instructions and know when to carry out the best strategy with a "sixth sense" of discernment. We also need strong heart instincts along with the bravery to execute orders at a moment's notice. In addition, we must also develop well-tuned ears to know when to march forward and when to wait. It takes extensive practice to maintain this delicate, multifaceted balance.

Single-minded soldiers also cannot process information as simply as many people do. Most people tend to read words, assign categories to the words and then send them to the appropriate mental file cabinet. The categories range from "fact" to "fiction" with hundreds of subtitles between.

Just like the military soldier, we as Christians have to be trained to reposition our thinking and process thoughts in a new way—a spiritual way. Let's look at the insights from spiritual giant to get a deeper explanation of how this process works.

In Oswald Chambers' sermon, "The Radical Region of Life," he refers to the heart as the "Radiator of Personal Life." Chambers says: *"Thinking takes place in the heart, not the brain. The real spiritual powers of a man reside in the heart, which is the center of the physical life, of the soul life, and of the spiritual life."*

I believe he is also saying that the choices we make with the information we gather are to be made in the heart, not the head. Our brains must first read the words and process them. Once words are understood by the intellect, a decision needs to be made. For the Christian, that decision must be made spiritually, in the heart.

The Bible says, *"For the Word of God...is a discerner of the thoughts and intents of the **heart"*** (Hebrews 4:12, KJV). Notice the verse says the heart—**not the head!**

The decisions that we make in the heart construct who we are, and they determine what we will become. Unlike the old saying, *we are not what we read. Rather, we are what we "decide to do" with what we have read.*

Paul instructs us to be careful about how we "build" with what we learn. *"According to the grace (the special endowment for my task) of God bestowed on me, like a skillful architect and master builder I, (Paul) laid [the] foundation, and now another [man] is building upon it. But let each [man] be careful how he builds upon it"* (1 Corinthians 3:10, AMPC). It is our responsibility to build correctly; therefore, a good understanding of the blueprints we read is absolutely imperative. Then, what we decide to do with the information we receive becomes the way the construction is actually executed.

Paul also tells us more about how obedience plays a vital role in thinking with our heart. *"But thank God, though you were once slaves of sin, you have become **obedient with all your heart to the standard of teaching** in which you were instructed (head) and to which you were committed, (heart)"* (Romans 6:17, AMPC, bold emphasis from this author).

Notice that an obedient *heart* comes after *intellect in the head*, which is "the standard of teaching." So be careful what you listen to and what you read.

Many years ago, I got convicted about what I was listening to on the radio when I drive. I was always listening to either mind-numbing music or bad news. What I heard not only wasted my time, but it was also depressing. So, I made up my mind to give my "car-time" to the Lord. I decided to only listen to godly things like Gospel music, teaching and preaching.

Realizing that not all "Gospel" stations are created equal, I said a prayer to protect myself before I even started the car. The prayer I used was a short one—something like: *"Lord, keep me from hearing anything that is not right. Help me remember all that is right, and conform my heart and mind according to the truth as I am led by your Spirit."*

(Even though this prayer is short, if you decide to pray it while you are driving in the car, I suggest you keep your eyes open.)

The same prayer should be considered when you are watching television, reading books or spending time on the Internet. Remember this: there are only two gates to your mind—the eye-gate and the ear-gate. Both should be protected.

These concepts about the head and heart are vitally important in understanding how salvation really works. Those who have only a superficial understanding of salvation may have had it explained to them as simply a "belief." They believe that there is a God and that Jesus was His Son. They may even believe that Jesus came to this earth as a man, died and rose again. He rose from the dead so that all could escape God's judgment and go to Heaven instead of Hell. That's all they believe there is to the God thing—Bata-Bing, Bata-Boom—done, they are finished! Check that off the list and move on.

Well, hold up there, lead dog! While everything mentioned about belief is absolutely true, it is not the whole enchilada of salvation by any stretch. Belief is only a shadow of the whole truth. It is not enough to have knowledge or an intellectual understanding of what you believe to be true. Rather, what counts is what you did with the knowledge and understanding that you obtained about salvation. The act of salvation is actually implemented when you ask the Spirit of God to take your intellect and move it about 18 inches south—to your heart—and you commit to it. You may have heard the saying: "Things are better in the South." Well, this principle is one of those things!

In the very moment that we **commit to act on** God's gift of salvation (in other words at the time that we have intellectually understood salvation, have come to believe it to be true and decided to act upon it), we **receive** it. We ask to receive it because of a fixed determination and a commitment on our part to take God up on His offer to save us. We figuratively extend our hand and place it in His already out-stretched hand as if to say, *"I'll take it! Let's shake on it."*

The "deal" is accomplished by God through His Son by the power of His Spirit. This receiving of this gift is explained very well in the Amplified version of the Bible in this very familiar verse:

*"For God so greatly loved and dearly prized the world that He [even] gave up His only begotten (unique) Son, so that whoever **believes in, (trusts in, clings to, relies on)** Him shall not perish (come to destruction, be lost) but have eternal (everlasting) life"* (John 3:16, AMPC, bold emphasis from this author).

I suggest you read that verse again. Right after the word, "believes," insert these thoughts to ensure your belief is complete:

1) Because I have heard about this great love that God has for me.
2) Because I intellectually understand what salvation was about and why it was necessary.
3) Because I understand that it was a free gift available to me.

Here is what I'd like you to see as you examine this verse. First *your intellectual understanding requires you to make a decision based on what you now understand and "believe" to be true.* Then, after the believing part comes the commitment part. That's the part where you "trust in, cling to and rely on." Faith moves the intellect south, into your heart, and your heart fully trusts that God will do what He said He would. Your faith commits to the offer and the Spirit of God seals it!

And, because you are totally committed to the promise attached, *"You will not perish but have everlasting life!"*

I'll bet you have to read that more than once. But this process is critical. You must understand how salvation works. The "nutshell" is: we have intellectually heard about salvation; it's because we freely choose to do something about what we have come to understand; and we commit to receive what God has already provided and paid for in advance.

You see, it doesn't matter how well a gift is wrapped and presented. Nor does it matter how sincere the giver is or how convinced you are that the present is indeed a gift intended for you. The fact of the matter is that a gift is not yours until **you** accept it. The decision to accept or reject a gift is your responsibility. That decision requires you to take hold of it, in faith, and claim it as your own.

Let me give you another example that might be a bit easier to understand.

Do you believe that any major airline has the ability to fly you to Paris, France? Do you believe that the airlines have the aircraft, the pilots, the experience and the fuel to get you there safely? If you believe that, then answer this question: Why are you not in Paris right now? You "believe" it's possible, don't you?

You aren't there yet because a "belief" is just something you believe to be true. It doesn't "do" anything. Your simple belief cannot help you get to Paris. A commitment and action must take place for you to actually get there. You must book the flight, show up at the airport and board the plane. When you sit down and strap in to your designated seat, you have placed your faith and trust in that airline to do what you "believed" they could do.

Once you are in the plane, your trip is no longer just something you believe could happen, it is a fact: you ARE going! And I might add, I fully expect you to be committed to stay on board till you arrive at your destination! Don't change your mind somewhere over the Atlantic!

On the flip side, a simple belief that poison will kill you if you drink it, doesn't make you dead. A belief alone cannot hurt you either. You would have to commit to drinking poison for it to do any damage.

The gift of salvation is offered to everyone. Belief by itself is just a shadow of what salvation is. To be single-minded soldiers for Christ, the first step is understanding this foundational truth of receiving this gift. True and complete salvation is a **heart** decision that cannot be left out, or you too will be…left behind.

2.

How to Read with Your Head, but Think with Your Heart: Part 2

Strengthening Strategy:
Understanding what you are s*aved "from" and saved "to"—conditional and unconditional covenants.*

In the last chapter, we used a few words and phrases like: "finished" and "done deal" when we talked about the basic belief in the gift of salvation. But I'm afraid that there is a bit more to the Christian life than initial salvation. We need to know more about the next step of working out our salvation, or building Christ-like character, to carry out our marching orders as strategic, single-minded soldiers.

I am going to go a little more in depth in this chapter, but for some, it may seem a bit elementary. Some readers may not know much about this second step at all. And yet, working and living out our salvation is critical and fundamental to successfully living a life that is pleasing to God. So, for those of us who need to hear a little, cut us some spiritual slack and allow more heavenly latitude, please!

If you study the Bible or attend church with any regularity, you will discover that there are many covenant promises of God. Salvation is just one of them. Basically, there are two different kinds of covenants: "unconditional" and "conditional."

An "unconditional" covenant promise means that this promise is *going to take place*, period! For example, God told Abraham that He was *going* to make a great nation out of him.

He did not come to Abraham and ask him what he thought about the idea. He did not ask Abraham to do anything in particular to make this promise come to pass. He didn't even ask Abraham if he was interested in the idea. God had determined what He was going to do and God made the decision known to Abraham.

Other covenant promises are "conditional," which means that they have a prerequisite, or condition, that must be fulfilled *before* the covenant is in effect. Salvation is a conditional covenant promise that demands a commitment. In fact, salvation requires an initial commitment **and** an "on going" commitment.

In the previous chapter, I explained, based on the Scripture, how salvation is obtained. If you are saved, you are assured that you are going to heaven when you die. That promise is guaranteed.

What should we be doing from the time we accept the gift and commit to Christ until our ultimate arrival in heaven? Should we sin like crazy because we are locked into going to heaven? Common sense tells us obviously not to do that.

If you believe you can keep sinning and still live the Christian life effectively, you're not only in the wrong church and pew, you aren't even in the right zip code!

Just like our salvation is not a license to sin because our final destination is secure, our salvation is not a license to sit down and do nothing until we die either. A person who has truly been redeemed (or saved) by Jesus Christ will not live a life characterized by continuous sin. Nor will they lead a slothful and uneventful existence. They will want to work, share and live for Christ.

When you become "saved," there should be some significant evidence of that change, both immediate and long-term. You should be uncomfortable with doing some of the activities you used to do, and you should not want to go to some of the places you used to go.

Something inside you finds that those activities and places that previously seemed fine are now contrary to your new way of thinking. This difference in your feelings is a great confirmation that you have indeed received a new life, because the desire to do the activities you did in the old life is now gone.

In addition, the feeling you have when you do something

wrong is God's Holy Spirit placing you in check. The exhilaration you feel when you do something right is the affirmation of God's Holy Spirit. He is your guide now and He will nudge you in the right direction.

You see, it's not enough to hit the ball out of the park— you still have to run the bases before you can put the score on the board. Salvation alone hits it out of the park—in terms of saving you from eternal separation from God and making it possible for you to have an abundant life here. However, you still have to fulfill your commitment. You have to run around the bases and cross home plate.

The Bible tells us what a saved person does in this verse: *"Who is a wise man and endued [given to or blessed with* (added by this writer)] *with knowledge among you? Let him shew [demonstrate, live* (added by this writer)] *out of a good conversation his **works** with meekness of wisdom"* (James 3:13, KJV).

In this context, we are *not* talking about "**a work,**" (singular) as in "earning" our salvation. We are talking about "**works**" (plural) that are a "result of" our salvation.

Part of that journey toward our ultimate, heavenly destination requires this kind of character-building **work.** That is, "living out," or being what we say we have become, while we are still here. The bottom line is that a person's life from salvation to heaven should be full of good **works.** James is saying that these **works** should constantly and consistently provide credible evidence of who you have become.

Character building works are not merely a **collection** of isolated actions or impulsive reactions that affect the direction of our life as we move forward. Instead, character building is a lifelong process and commitment to hard work. God wants us to be committed in advance to what He will ask us to do, rather than simply react to situations as they come up.

God is more interested in helping you imitate His Son's character than He is expanding yours.

God wants us to make Christ-like selections as we decide how to use our time. He wants us to choose activities each day like praying, reading the Bible, attending church, loving people and doing good works. He is interested in us making good selections as a result of commitment, not simply accumulating a collection of experiences.

An example of making a good selection would be to commit not to drink well in advance of something bad happening while driving a car. Conversely, a simple reaction to wrongful actions would be to make the decision to stop drinking *after* multiple DUI's, a bad car wreck and serving jail time.

How do we do make a dramatic shift after salvation? How do we all-of-a-sudden make good decisions and selections? How do we know the difference? As the Bible says: *"He who has an ear, let him hear"* (Revelation 3:6, NIV). This verse is not talking about the ability to hear physically. Rather, those of you who have spiritual ears, (which you have now that you are saved) listen spiritually to what He will reveal through the Holy Spirit.

Likewise, those of you who have spiritual eyes (eyes that now see spiritually), let him read with and gain spiritual insight from God's perspective. Listening and seeing spiritually enable you to properly select in your **heart** what is right. This process is building Christ-like character.

Did you notice that we are back to the **"heart"** position again? Accepting salvation is understood in the head but decided in the **heart**. Christ-like character building is also first understood by studying and learning about Jesus' life. But it is accomplished (worked out, becomes real) in the **heart**. It becomes the heart's desire to be more like Him and less like who we used to be.

When we become saved, God makes our new heart's desire possible by giving us spiritual gifts. These gifts are vital to us doing what He expects. He gives us spiritual eyes so that we can see matters from his perspective. He provides spiritual ears so that we can hear directly from Him by His Spirit. These gifts—spiritual eyes, spiritual ears and a spiritually transformed heart are the tools necessary to living the Christian Life. But these gifts must be developed with practice, time and effort.

The bottom line of these two chapters is that we are saved "FROM" Hell and saved "TO" live a life that demonstrates that we have indeed been saved. Our life becomes fruitful for all to see. Our successful growth is revealed by the power of God being released in and through our obedient, God directed, hard "**work**." This work is a result of God building a "single-minded," Christ-like disciple.

Perhaps the most amazing aspect of the whole head and heart working together is that God actually does all the work. Our job as single-minded solders is to choose to allow Him to do the work through us. His power and work through us is what keeps our Christian legacy from becoming a shadow of what God intended it to be.

Seeing this living proof lived out through the life of transformed people (or single-minded soldiers) is what encourages others to find out what happened to enable such a change to take place.

As people observe our lives first hand, they will come to want what we have. Therefore, carrying out the marching orders and living our lives for Christ is helping others to keep from being...left behind.

3.
Prayer, Meditation...or Both?

Strengthening Strategy:
Using spiritual eyes, spiritual ears and more.

We have a desire in our heart to live a life that is pleasing to God. We also understand that we are expected to do good works. But, how do we develop the ability to know what to do and what not to do? How do we gain the understanding of how to carry out our instructions correctly?

A single-minded soldier listens to his commander, and makes sure that he can hear his orders. As Christians, to execute our orders from Jesus, our Commander, we must also depend on two important activities: **prayer** and **meditation.**

It is not enough just to prayerfully read or speak words, but we must meditate on them. Neither should we just meditate and forget to prayerfully ask for events to come about. Are you confused yet? Let me define prayer and meditation to help clear things up.

Prayer is asking God to put into motion things that are not happening...until you ask. Prayer is also asking God to reveal his will to you. **Meditation** often includes prayer, but it is not prayer.

Meditation is the power of the heart to understand and process the details of a subject accurately. You may have to read verses and meditate on them to get the whole story **as you pray** and ask God to implement the truth into your **heart.**

We must not only be willingly to receive a specific "work order" from God, but we also need to ask Him to put the plan in motion through prayer. Then, we need to gather and learn about the supporting steps that may be required to actually carry the order out through meditation.

Throughout the Bible, you will often see prayer and meditation used together in the same sentence. Sometimes, they will be in the reverse order. However, the underlying principle is that they generally go together. They are actually two sides of the same coin.

Let me give you an example;

- Is it good to cross the street if you have prayed about it and feel led to do so? Yes.
- Is it better to cross the street at a crosswalk? Yes, because that makes it legal.
- Is it okay to cross the street if I don't hear or see anything coming? Yes, because the street being clear is a prerequisite to crossing safely.

After you answer these questions affirmatively, you are totally "led," "legal" and "prepared" to cross the street. All of a sudden, as you **meditate (ponder, consider and judge the worth of it and reflect...)**, it dawns on you that:

- You left the stove on.
- You forgot to tell your family where you are going and when you will return.
- You are still in your pajamas.

I think the crossing needs to be delayed a bit, don't you? It doesn't exactly look like the right time to do the right thing—even though you were "led," "legal" and "prepared" to do it.

You may have received instructions in prayer to do something very specific. However, meditating on these instructions may reveal some details about how and when to implement them. So, what does meditation tell us? It tells us that timing is every bit as important as the commitment that you have made to obey.

We now have the formula and the tools for obedient Christian living, which develops Christ-like character. Let's think of this process—also known as sanctification—as a simple mathematical equation:

If you take reading (having spiritual eyes to see heavenly things) and add: hearing (spiritual ears to hear from God), and add: praying (asking and listening for direction), and add: *meditating (consider the details, pondering) you get:* the perfect answer for successful, obedient service!

We must learn what to do, how to do it and when to do it! The "spiritual" tools and the entire formula of asking, receiving and carrying out our "orders" come from a heart's desire and firm commitment to please God.

We want to live a life that demonstrates that we are part of His unit. We say that we have become a "Christian," which means, "Christ-like." So, when we obey using both the formula and the tools to become more "Christ-like," we give God the highest act of worship and praise. We will also have developed into single-minded soldiers, who think and act like God's Son, Jesus. The result will be a desire to obey orders EXACTLY like Jesus—in every way, every day, all the time—without exception.

Christ himself spoke of His own heart's desire: *"I am able to do nothing from Myself [independently, of My own accord—but only as I am taught by God and as I get His orders]. Even as I hear, I judge [I decide as I am bidden to decide. As the voice comes to Me, so I give a decision], and My judgment is right (just, righteous), because I do not seek or consult My own will [I have no desire to do what is pleasing to Myself, My own aim, My own purpose] but only the will and pleasure of the Father Who sent Me"* (John 5:30, AMPC).

Aren't Jesus' words amazing? Here we are at the "heart" again. It was the Son's heart's desire to do the will of his Father.

In addition to Jesus' words, do you know what is also amazing? It is amazing to me that science confirms what the Bible says. Science tells us that the first organ that is formed and fully functional in physical birth is the heart. The baby's heart actually begins to beat about 18 days after conception. You can actually hear it at about eight weeks.

Salvation (new birth or Spiritual birth) begins with the **heart**, which is also the first thing that must be re-born. *"Ye must be born again"* (John 3:7, KJV). So, it is a wonderful thing that God can cleanse and purify the thinking of our newly birthed *hearts*. This cleansing of the heart determines what we say and how we act. That is why the Lord says, *"Of the abundance of the **heart**, his mouth speaketh"* (Luke 6:45, KJV*)*.

Just as our *physical* heart is the most critical organ of our human life, our *spiritual* heart is the most critical part of a new life in Christ. Once our spiritual heart is conceived in Christ, it begins to function in the most elementary way.

Then, other spiritual tools begin to develop. We already discussed eyes to see with and ears to hear. But we also need spiritual fingers to work and spiritual feet to take us where we need to go. Our entire bodies were designed by God to allow our hearts to do what they decide to do. If we have been saved, we are equipped to live like we were intended to live…spiritually.

My prayer is that the words in this book come from my spirit-controlled heart and are read by those who want, or now have, spiritual eyes. I pray that the individuals who read it will make it their spiritual heart's desire to please God and do good works using both prayer and meditation.

No matter where we are on our spiritual journey, we all must continually process information on how to live out an obedient life. I pray that we will commit or recommit with our hearts to "trust in, cling to and rely on" (again, John 3:16) the perfect word, work and will of God.

To become focused and well trained single-minded soldiers, Christians must continually work to develop all of our minds, bodies and spirits to live lives that we now claim to have. As our minds stay focused, our actions will carry out God's orders. We will then be the substance rather than a shadow of Christianity. Then, nothing that God wants for us—or for those He wants us to bless—will be left out.

4.

The Dangers of Juicing

Strengthening Strategy:
Maintaining the purity of the Gospel message.

On my quest to become the best single-minded soldier I could be, I decided I needed to improve my physical health as well. To that end, about two years ago, my wife and I bought a "juicer." That's a turbo-charged blender for making food-mush. This contraption is sold with promises to transform all the things that are good for you—and that naturally taste terrible—into drinkable delights.

With a juicer, you quickly learn a few tricks to make the juice more palatable—like adding apples. Here's how juicing works: First, you throw everything you want in the juicer. Then, just add an apple, and presto! It makes that green, slimy, pond-scum-like substance taste much sweeter so that it goes down a little easier. In addition, the chances of the pond scum staying down there are greatly increased.

Adding extra ingredients to make the Gospel taste better is what some churches, evangelists and pastors are doing as well. They are "juicing" the Gospel.

The problem with "Gospel juicing" is that once you start, you have a tendency to add more things and leave other things out to make it even better, less boring and more like what we really want...a religious milkshake!

When I first started juicing, I was hard-core. I was a totally committed, die hard, honest juicer. I was destined to become the Superman of Slime and Slush, the Patriarch of Pungent Punch, the…well, you get the idea. I juiced everything I could find—and down it went! I was determined to set the pace for my wife and then watch to see if she could keep up.

On the second day, I started to add sweetener, honey, nuts, peanut butter and finally the magic bullet…chocolate! One full week into the juicing thing and I was only making fruit smoothies and milkshakes. Everything got confusing, but I was convinced I was doing a good thing. Unfortunately, I just continued the downward spiral of compromise, satisfied my cravings and gained weight. There it was…"compromised juicing." I was just going through the motions, and I ended up juicing myself right back into belly-fat city.

Our motivation to live out our version of Christianity can be just like my initial juicing experience—short-lived and compromised—especially if we don't seem to object to compromised juicing of the Gospel. We can be determined and focused when we are first saved to live for Christ no matter what, but little-by-little, the recipe gets mixed up and the whole truth can become altered and diluted.

Two stipulations of the Gospel that I believe have been "juiced" warrant our attention, because they are the most critical.

These two key issues are **salvation** and **grace.** If we can get a pure understanding of these two concepts, it will bring many other issues into focus. We will continue to explore salvation here; grace will be addressed in a later chapter.

"Saved," possessing salvation or knowing, believing and living for Christ, is a term we use to distinguish us from being "lost," or living without knowing, believing and living for Christ. If either one of these terms is altered, the true meaning of each cannot be understood correctly, and the vision of both is skewed at best. If the view is skewed enough, it is possible to miss the point entirely, even with the best of intensions.

Nothing is between being lost and being saved. If a person is saved, as we learned earlier, they will spend eternity in Heaven, which is filled with God's glory. If they are lost, they will be tormented eternally in the fires of Hell, a place void of God and any goodness. The eternal destination of people is why the accuracy, content and substance of the message of salvation must be preserved and shared.

If not, many people will be juiced by a culturally more palatable, watered-down version of Christianity, but they will remain lost and…left behind.

5.

Grace Du Jour

Strengthening Strategy:
Receiving the offer of introductory grace—pure and simple, but accurate.

OK, single-minded soldiers, let's recap! We have gone through our training examining the need for salvation and the way to receive salvation. We followed that with looking at the tools and formula that God gives us once we were saved to live out our salvation. Then we discussed the dangers of "juicing" the Gospel.

Let's move to the next step and take a look at the grace of God, which is the reason salvation can be offered to sinful humans in the first place. We will also discuss how the grace of God also gets "juiced" and served on the "easy platter" of compromise.

We have learned that being saved gets us to the ultimate destination of Heaven and provides us a path to an abundant, peaceful life on Earth. We have also seen that Jesus is the only path that we can take to be saved. It is the grace of God, however, that provides the passport and pays for the ticket for our journey.

In the next two chapters, we will look at two important and inseparable aspects of grace. These two inseparable aspects of grace are intricately weaved into the fabric of salvation.

The first aspect of grace is what we will call, "introductory grace," which intrigues us and invites us to come to God. The other facet of grace is "saving grace," which takes us through His door and seals the transaction forever.

We will not attempt to cover the entirety of the grace of God in this book. Grace is not just a simple, generic, all-encompassing term referring to the generosity of God. It would take volumes to even scratch the surface of the topic of God's amazing grace.

Hopefully, this explanation of just two aspects of God's grace will help you understand it in an introductory way. And, at the same time, I hope that it will entice you to go deeper into a study of grace. I promise, the more you know about grace, the more you will want to know.

To get a good understanding of how important it is to keep these two aspects of grace precise, the next time you bake a cake, substitute corn starch for flour and see what you get. OK, you don't have to bake, I'll tell you what happens: you end up with one flat, bitter dessert that you can only use as a door stop or a Frisbee.

Similarly, if you substitute a key ingredient in grace, you end up with a shadow of what grace really is and you don't understand what grace does. In some churches, this grace-du-jour purée is actually being served from the pulpit weekly or on television weakly. Get it? Weakly and weekly...anyway, pay attention—you missed a good one.

Some well-meaning churches and other ministries make this purée of grace seem like pretty good juice. It sounds good, looks good, taste good and it goes down easily. The problem is that just having a "juiced," one-sided relationship with Christ will not get you into Heaven. People who thought they had it right, may not realize that they have been juiced with the wrong formula, until it is too late.

Let's take a closer look at the **introductory** part of grace. John Wesley, the founder of the Methodist Church, refers to it as "prevenient grace." In modern English, the phrase "preceding or introductory grace" would have a similar meaning. Wesley says: *"It is my opinion that prevenient grace is that portion of grace that is made available to* **everyone***. 'Whosoever will, may come' is true."*

John Wesley was explaining that God will give everyone will an opportunity to hear and respond to the invitation to be saved.

Just because the invitation is given to everyone, however, does not mean that everyone will receive the invitation in exactly the same way. We are individuals and the introduction to God's grace by His Holy Spirit will be uniquely tailored to your understanding at the exact time and place God chooses to reveal it to you. But, make no mistake, you will have received this invitation sometime, some way, during your lifetime—that's a promise of God!

I have studied this concept for years and have come to the clear understanding that *"introductory grace" is the stepping stone that leads to the second portion of grace that we will discuss, which is known as "saving grace."*

I might add, that ultimately, we will experience "eternal grace" in Heaven forever. But that is a topic for another time. I just want to remind you that grace never stops working and that it has many facets to it. Like a gemstone, each facet is designed to enhance the entire stone by bringing more light and life to it.

From the first introduction of grace, to the final realization of grace in Heaven for eternity, God's grace is at work. First, it saves, then it protects and leads in this life, and ultimately it secures our heavenly promise for all eternity. All this work is done by the God's varying facets of His truly amazing grace.

Now, let's step back from the theological terms a little and explain both aspects of grace with an analogy that may be easier for us to grasp.

Let's use "love" and "marriage" to draw a parallel. (Unfortunately, love and marriage are not always related, but for the sake of this discussion, we will assume that they are.)

From our first loves in grade school and high school proms to "e-harmony" or "farmers only.com," we are on a quest to find Mr. or Miss "Right."

We do a lot of shopping because we are not exactly sure what we are looking for in a partner. We just know that something internally drives us toward the discovery, the romance and ultimate conquest of true love. *(Is anyone else seeing the beginning of a Hallmark movie?)* Anyway, sometimes love is a result of hard work and diligent searching. Sometimes, it just sneaks up on you when you are not even looking and...Bata-Bing, Bata-Boom...your dreamboat arrives at the dock!

I clearly remember chasing my wife until she caught me. It was a glorious achievement for us both. (Not everyone is as fortunate as we are at 43 years of marriage and counting!)

The love relationship with God is different from the love of human relationships. God's grace-love is so great that He decided that no one would be left off the "A" list. In fact, he determined that everyone would receive the same invitation with his or her individual name on it. And, the invitation would be offered to each one of us because of the wonderful, initial, introductory part of God's wonderful grace—without any effort or cost on our part.

This introductory invitation may first come in the form of an intellectually discovery through what is read or heard. It may be accompanied by a feeling inside that can't be quite described. Perhaps you will feel it during a song, a poem or a sermon. But make no mistake—it will come, and you will know it.

This invitation is one incredible, heavenly promise! You **will**, (not may, or could or should) receive this introductory invitation because no one is "left off" of His "A" list.

Caution! As wonderful as that sounds, his invitation is a double-edged sword that demands a response. But, if you do not respond correctly—if you don't commit to accept His Lordship in your life and be His single-minded soldier, you will most assuredly be...left out of life in Heaven.

6.
Grace Realized

Strengthening Strategy:
Appropriating saving grace…two sides of the same coin?

In the previous chapter, we discussed how the message of salvation was presented to us through the introductory invitation of the grace of God.

We also stated that it was not enough to be introduced, but that the introduction expects and demands a response.

If all my prospective wife would have received from me was an introductory nod or an intellectual acknowledgement, she would have missed the opportunity of a lifetime of bliss, romance, travel, excitement—and of course, chocolate—on a regular basis. She needed a response, and I had to take action before all of her wildest dreams could actually be realized.

Our relationship with God is similar but with much greater reward **OR** more severe, eternal consequences. It is your choice. You see, everyone has eternal life—they just need to decide where they are going to spend it.

By now, you may be wondering if we can be saved without knowing all these details about the grace of God. Satan is the great deceiver. We must be single-minded and deeply focused on this eternal issue, so stay with me…

The saving grace of God gives us permission to actually pursue a relationship with Him. Receiving the introductory invitation without saving grace would have been akin to meeting your future wife briefly—and that's it. She is simply an acquaintance, and the relationship with her never progresses. You experience no romance, no intimacy, no planning, no growing or enjoying each other.

During the romance of getting from the initial introduction to walking down the aisle with my beloved, I got asked and gave answers to some very important questions: *Why do you love me? Why do we want to get married? What are your plans for a future? What do you expect of me? How long could our marriage last? Do you want a family?*

You should know these answers before you ever commit to marry someone. If you uncover these revelations after you are married, you may experience a great deal of stress, frustration, separation or even divorce.

So, as I have said—but, just to review: God's saving grace is all about romance, but it is very different in its application and timing than marriage between a man and woman is. God's relationship offer is better because you don't have to—nor do you do need to—know all the answers before you commit to Him. He allows you to gradually discover all that your commitment involves as you progress in your guaranteed, irrevocable, unending, ever-increasing love relationship called salvation.

If He required you to know everything about His love and saving grace prior to your relationship, you would never get there. It would take a thousand forevers. And, His love and grace bestowed upon you at salvation would not be "unmerited" gifts either—and they certainly are.

Salvation is all about saving you "from" the wrath and judgment of God. God's grace is also about saying yes "to" what he has in store for you. He offers a love relationship that you cannot begin to comprehend **until** you start down the path with Him.

God's grace is the explanation of how salvation happened and why it happened. You were saved because God loved you in advance. Then, God's Spirit drew you. He urged, encouraged and pursued you. In His "introductory grace" he helped you understand enough in your heart to decide what you needed to do with His invitation.

Then, when you answered the invitation with an eternal "yes," God's "saving grace" took over. By the power of God's Spirit, He sealed the deal. It was done. Welcome aboard, cast off the ropes, blow the whistle...we are about to set sail!

So, below is a brief recap of our scratch-the-surface understanding of just two facets of God's grace. It is something that we as Christians will be uncovering a little more each day for the rest of our earthly lives. Only when we are face-to-face with Him in Heaven, will we receive a complete understanding of His amazing, multifaceted grace-love for us.

God's introductory grace:
- Makes us aware of the need to be saved.
- Shows us the "way" to receive it.
- Draws us by His Spirit.
- Extends the invitation to us,

and if we say yes to his invitation,

God's saving grace:
- Is invoked by an act of our will by faith.
- Seals our relationship with God forever until we experience eternal grace in Heaven.

The other aspects of the grace of God include protection, provision and much more. But for now, it is important for us to know that we have been saved and kept by these initial parts of the grace of God.

Now that we are saved, He has a job for us to do, and that job always involves getting to know Him better. We need to grow in our knowledge of Him and share His love and truth with others. We must get to work—not to earn what we already have (salvation), but to live out what we claim we are!

Now it's time for the real romance to begin. If we don't get the foundation right in this relationship, no matter what we build from that point forward, it will only be a *shadow* of what it could and should be.

This new relationship of knowing and loving God and sharing his love and truth with others are two of the most important parts to your Grace relationship. Knowing and sharing His love are the core of His plan and purpose for every single-minded soldier...and they must not be...left behind.

7.

Ignorance Is Not Bliss

Strengthening Strategy:
Delaying the inevitable casts shadows on the truth.

As a single-minded soldier, you must thoroughly understand your directive or you could make a decision that adversely affects someone's life with eternal consequences. Complete understanding and strict obedience to your marching orders will keep casualties to a minimum.

In spiritual matters, you will find yourself in a position to ask others the question, *"Do you know how you get to Heaven?"* Or, you may pose it a different way and say: *"How do you become saved?"* Chances are, you will probably get as many different answers as the number of people you ask.

The answers will range from a superficial and generic answer of *"just being good"* to the basic and honest response of *"I don't have a clue."* Some may think that they will die and come back as someone or something else. (If that's the case, I know a few people that will probably be a June bug on someone's windshield.)

One thing is for sure. If you ask the question, *"Do you want to go to Heaven after this life?"* The answer will most certainly be, *"Yes."* What is sad is that although everyone wants to go Heaven, very few people have the GPS locator to get there.

You may even be asked, *"Why do we even have to 'do' anything to get to Heaven anyway? If God loves us all, why doesn't He just let everyone in? After all, sending people to Hell is not a very loving thing to do."*

In the third chapter of the Gospel of John, Nicodemus was

told that in order for him to go to Heaven, he had to be born again. All Nicodemus knew about being "born" was limited to physical birth. This idea of "spiritual rebirth" had to be explained to him. We also need to explain it correctly if we are going to expect others to understand the necessity of it.

Being "spiritually reborn," which is synonymous with "saved," is part of God's plan of salvation, and it is free to every man. "The Way" (the only way) that you become spiritually born again is through a person, Jesus, God's Son. Being saved is not just a direction or a goal, it is a holy prerequisite to get to Heaven. You become born again, saved, by believing in and accepting God's plan called grace through his Son, Jesus—or you don't get in, period!

Jesus said, speaking to His disciple Thomas, *"I am the way, the truth, and the life. No one comes to the Father except through Me" (John 14:6, NKJV).*

The only bridge over the holy chasm between God and the sin of man is Jesus. It is not enough for people just to know that there is a separation problem—they need to know that there is a separation solution. They need to know there is a "Way" and they need to know "who" the "Way" is.

When we share with others about the "Way" to salvation, we must understand that you cannot convince someone that they need to be saved unless they first understand that they are "lost" or unsaved. They must clearly see they are going the wrong way.

Have you ever wondered why in some instances, people prefer ignorance over knowledge? I believe there are several reasons for this misconception. The first one is that if they are ignorant about something, they feel they don't have to deal with it.

For instance, someone may be facing a fatal health issue, but they will ignore the symptoms or seeing a doctor because they are fearful of the diagnosis. They prefer not to know, rather than to find out the facts about what's happening. It's as if not knowing would somehow change the outcome. In actuality, it only delays the inevitable. Eventually, when people are finally forced to address their medical problems, their situations can be much worse.

People's tendency to plead ignorance is probably the reason that the saying, "Ignorance of the law is no defense," came about. That saying means that just because you did not know there was a law against spitting on the sidewalk, does not excuse you from obeying the law. (By-the-way guys, you shouldn't be dating women that do that anyway—it's a disgusting habit!)

Likewise, people not knowing about the judgment that they will face when they die, doesn't give them a justifiable excuse before God. Therefore, people must face the fact that they have an eternal life problem before they will ever consider listening to an eternal life solution.

This "ignorance is bliss" mentality reminds me of a potential life scenario: A couple is finally going on a much-needed vacation after a very stressful year. They have been traveling in the car for about an hour when the wife says to her husband. *"Do you realize that we are going in the wrong direction?"* He answers, *"Yes, I know that, but we are making such good time. I hate to turn around!"*

I think that because so many people today are so stressed, confused and pressured, it is hard for them to make room for anything new—even if it has eternal consequences. As long as they are busy and working hard, they believe they are making progress. They don't even seem to care if they are going in the wrong direction. They don't seem to be bothered if they are unprepared for the longest trip that they will ever make—to eternity!

As single-minded soldiers, it is up to us to make everyone who we come in contact with aware of the fact that they may be headed toward eternal disaster. They must come to understand that ignorance is not bliss, and we must help them see that they are about to be…left behind.

8.
The "KISS" Principle

Strengthening Strategy:
Keeping It Simple Saint—Is it supply and demand or demand to supply?

Because most people are not naturally laser focused like a sales superstar or a high-powered executive, it may be difficult for them to find the courage to initiate a conversation about faith in Jesus or to defend their beliefs. Perhaps they have trouble gathering their thoughts together about the saving grace of God through Jesus. Maybe they have even more difficulty finding the right opportunity to deliver this message to others.

Those challenges don't even account for the arduous task of mustering up enough courage to ask someone to make a decision to accept Christ and receive His gift of salvation. So, how do Christians who are not mission minded or sales oriented have these conversations?

This scenario is where the Christian "KISS" principle comes into play. The Christian "KISS" principle is: "**K**eep **I**t **S**imple, **S**aint."

Simple minds like to think in pictures and/or receive simple examples that they can relate to quickly.

(As previously stated, I am uniquely qualified to comment on many areas of life. Being simpleminded is just another attribute of mine, so let me give you some simple examples of what I mean about filling this need.)

We live in a country based on "supply and demand." Some of the demand is for what Americans consider basic survival "**needs**:"

clothing, housing, a job, chocolate, peanut butter, Pop Tarts—and a new car every three years. That's American success!

This type of "supply and demand" produces the supply based on the ever-increasing demand of the consumer. "Supply and demand" continues to work hand-in-hand in an unending circle at an ever-increasing rate as we progress. Yea for democracy and capitalism!

However, much of the demand today has been totally manufactured well **in advance** of any conscious demand by the consumer. Many things on our list of what we perceive as essential "needs" of a basic, successful lifestyle actually expands out of our activities, knowledge growth and selfish desires. Many other things that we buy were not even on our list. In fact, they weren't even in our dreams yet!

For example, smart phones were manufactured with the idea in mind that they would create a need in the consumers mind to match the supply that they wanted to sell. That mindset is completely opposite of what can be needed—creating a supply to meet a preexisting demand. It is routine procedure today to have a product completely manufactured, boxed up and ready to ship before it is even revealed to the world that it already exists. So, now we actually live in the age where "supply" actually creates the "demand" through advertising.

Dear Christian, do not miss this principle! This heavenly marketing plan is God's directive for you to pass on! We need to advise people that the "supply" has already been provided and the price has been paid before the demand was ever realized! That is the Gospel "smart" message! And yes, there's an **"app"** for that…already **p**aid **p**rice! (How do you like that one?)

The best way to help unbelievers see what their lives are like without God and what they will be like with God, is for them to examine your life. However, if the need arises and you have to do it with words, you can start with a few SIMPLE questions.

Here are just a few examples: *"Do you feel totally at peace? I don't mean, do you feel OK. But in every area of your life: body, soul, spirit, mind, emotion, and will, are you totally, complete, confident and at perfect peace? Do you have any doubts, apprehensions, fears, or even a slight thought that something is missing?"*

If they are honest, they would have to admit that something is just not right. More often than not, they have difficulty describing what that might be, or what they would do to make it better. But everything is not 100% OK in their lives. In fact, they are not even sure that idea of peace and rest is even possible in this world.

This part of the conversation is when you can explain why that uneasy feeling is there. They feel uneasy because every person who has ever breathed air has been born with a longing to know God. This void is implanted in everyone by God, and each of us must address this emptiness individually. In some way, somehow, someday, we will each be required to decide how to deal with that void. We will all make a decision to accept or reject the solution that God has. But, the question—the uneasiness—cannot be ignored. Nor is there any escape from the judgment that comes as a result of the wrong answer...it's just that simple.

The Apostle Paul explains: *"Because that which is known about God is evident within them [in their inner consciousness], for God made it evident to them. For ever since the creation of the world His invisible attributes, His eternal power and divine nature, have been clearly seen, being understood through His workmanship [all His creation, the wonderful things that He has made], so that they [who fail to believe and trust in Him] are without excuse and without defense"* (Romans 1:19–20, AMPC).

Once you get people to admit that the void exists, you have found the opportunity to explain it in detail. In Tennessee, we would say: *"Take those biscuits out of the oven, they are ready to be buttered!"* That's Heavenly Sales and Marketing 101—simple, easy and to the point!

Granted, you may meet someone who claims his life is all good. 100% OK...Life is a bowl of cherries and he has the spoon! Hmm, this guy is either easily pleased with no ambition or motivation for his future, or he is just blatantly dishonest. He is going to be a little harder nut to crack, and you may need a little bigger hammer.

In this case, try a different approach. Ask: *"So, if you were to die today, are you positive that you are going to Heaven?" "Are you sure that you have the right answer to give to God when He asks: 'What makes you think you qualify to come into my Heaven?'"*

The bottom line is that various types of people will give you various answers as you progress through the conversation, and you will be required to select different approaches.

The Spirit of God needs you to be sensitive toward His leading. Be prepared with your opening or introduction, but be equally ready to butter their bread no matter how they slice it. The single-minded soldier prepares in advance for adversity and opposition, and this opportunity is too important to leave to chance.

We will not spend time here to discuss all the aspects of witnessing because a couple thousand other books are already written on that subject. Your church may also offer this type of discipleship training. No matter how you receive this training, suffice it to say: It is your responsibility to find someone or some resource to help you get prepared.

Our world is in crisis mode. No matter where you look, people are in desperate need of hope and peace. They have accumulated truckloads of "stuff," and yet, they have no peace or joy.

Others need deliverance from issues, habits and addictions. All people need relief from the pressures, disappointments and frustrations of this life. All people need something better that the shadow substitutes or superficial explanations that won't provide lasting healing.

They need real, tangible solutions that give them blessed, eternal hope and clarity. They need to find the "way" to get the help and peace they need. They need a single-minded Christian soldier to take command and lead them. Keep It simple saint (KISS), but obey your orders from headquarters…and share the truth by being a witness with your own actions, words and deeds!

The supply has been provided, boxed up and delivered already. People just need to be made aware of their need.

Jesus is the ONLY "Way" that non-believers can have peace in this life. He is also the ONLY WAY they will not be…left behind, in the wrong place for eternity.

9.

The "Politically Correct" Gospel

Strengthening Strategy:
Determining what really needs to be left behind.

Single-minded Christian soldiers face many challenges. In addition to a hateful Enemy that wants to destroy them, they deal with opposition from society itself. Perverted concepts from people in positions of authority, as well as from teachers, politicians and the media, who want to limit what Christians say and do because someone may be offended.

We are asked to be more tolerant, or "politically correct." Time will tell how single-minded Christian soldiers will cope with this challenge, but our Ultimate Commander already has a plan to deal with this crazy notion. It is the Gospel of Jesus Christ and it is anything but "politically correct."

If we allow the Gospel to get juiced (as described in earlier chapters), everything else in our life becomes unclear, diluted and messy. God's Gospel by design is righteousness, peace and joy. But, when you add "politically correctness," everything we do and say becomes flawed, misdirected and unclear.

Sharing with others as we live our lives or as we intentionally witness to them becomes merely a **shadow** of what it should be.

What truly needs to be "left behind" is the notion that we can improve on the life-saving message of the Gospel. Any attempt to repackage it, paint it, bottle it or slice it is absolutely unacceptable.

The purity, totality and urgency of the message of grace is a sacred trust given to everyone who claims to be a child of God. Yet, attempts are made to water the Gospel down, sweeten it up and make it more convenient in the name of tolerance, compromise and convenience. This attempt is "political correctness" in action.

Those words are never used anywhere in the Bible nor are their close relatives: palatable, lazy, cheap and of course, *sensitive*. Well, lazy is referred to in what *not to be*! So, all of these words are, for Christians…"spiritually incorrect!"

The liberties we take with the sacred message of grace in trying to make it "politically correct" are way beyond appalling—they are dangerous because the misunderstanding of grace has eternal destination consequences! If you don't understand grace, you may not actually be saved! Even the slightest thought that the pure and simple grace message called the "Good News" might be altered in the smallest way, is blasphemy against Holy God! Some might think, "That's pretty strong language!" Well, the words need to be strong. I just hope they are strong enough.

The Gospel is Good News because it is holy news. Jesus Christ is the Son of God and the Savior of the world. That's great news! He is often described as *"the way where there seems to be no way."* And, that Good News is the only way to be certain you are not "left behind" and totally "left out" forever! You cannot mess with that truth!

In fact, that's not just good news as in the good of cream cheese icing on red velvet cake good—it is good as in heavenly good and supernaturally good. That kind of good doesn't get any better! That kind of good means eternal life with God—in Heaven, forever. That my friend, is PERFECT, HEAVENLY, GRACE-GOOD!

To take away from, to add to or to alter the Gospel message in any way, is the worst thing you could ever do to someone who is lost.

I remember my Dad telling me about a famous quote from C.S. Lewis, the famous theologian and author. Lewis said: *"The road to hell is paved with good intentions."* But in addition to being on that road, I think that some Christians, denominations and churches are also guilty of removing many of the warning signs along that road.

They may also repave the road with kind words to make the

trip smoother. They may widen the road to accommodate a larger variety of vehicles. And, they may even landscape the road to make it more attractive.

Then, they add more rest stops in case someone wants to stop traveling the road for a while. You know the type, those who *"take a sabbatical and start again later."* Or, even worse, are those who decide that they have been serving long enough and need a break. *"Let the younger ones take over now,"* they say…and on and on the excuses go.

Instead of getting diverted along the road side of our Christian life, God calls us to stay on course, to stay in our lanes and to never look back.

In addition to knowing Him better through His Word, praying and serving and others, Christians need God's sustaining grace. That grace provides continuous power and direction for the task ahead. We desperately need this power if we are to continue to carry out the mission that He gave us: delivering the Good News.

Our first responsibility as a single-minded Christian soldier from our Heavenly Commander is to obtain a basic, accurate understanding of the Gospel and to deliver it. We are never, ever to present a juiced, watered down or "politically correct" version of the Gospel.

The next step is to help the people that we shared that message with—now new believers—to find a church that teaches the Bible with the same, focused discipline that we just discussed.

Finally, we are to help new believers get properly trained, so that they can continue the process of learning about Christ. Then, they will be able to serve Him effectively.

This process of discipleship and walking alongside newer believers is God's mandate for our lives as single-minded Christian soldiers. We must make certain that everyone we meet hears and understands the Gospel with absolute clarity. We must do our part as single-minded soldiers to help ensure that others don't hear a "politically correct" Gospel. Otherwise they may be "left behind."

10.
Fulfilling the General Order

Strengthening Strategy:
Knowing some orders allow for innovation and flexibility; others do not.

The last command—that I call the "General Order" of the Lord—Jesus gave to His disciples before He ascended to Heaven: *"Go ye therefore, and teach all nations, baptizing them in the name of the Father and of the Son, and of the Holy ghost"* (Matthew 28:19, KJV).

These instructions were initially given more than 2,000 years ago. This "General Order," also known as The Great Commission, has not changed. It applies to us at this time in history just like it did then and it will apply until He comes again!

He instructs us all to proclaim the Good News with absolute truth, without apology, in total, unaltered, without reservation and to do it…**personally**!

I know that some of you were right with me until 1 I used the word, "personally." That's when your lunch tried to revolt and you broke into a cold sweat. Hang in there troops, we have an **app** for that too: **a**pplied **p**ersonal **p**articipation. (I'm getting good at these acronyms!)

The Bible tells us that as obedient instruments—as single-minded Christian soldiers—we can be used to pave the way for the Spirit of God to do His indispensable job. One of the main responsibilities of the Holy Spirit is to implement God's offer of salvation. He draws people to God's plan. He reveals the truth of it and, when they commit to receive it, by His power, He seals the agreement, forever!

Consider this "KISS" analogy that God created: God designed the vehicle that allows you to get you to Heaven. Jesus delivered the vehicle to you when He came to Earth. The Holy Spirit is the engine that provides the power to start you on your journey with God and the fuel to make the trip that you make throughout your life on Earth.

How does this analogy translate to us personally fulfilling God's General Order of going out and teaching about Him? Wherever we live or go—or whatever we do—our lives should demonstrate God's plan of salvation, which includes a well-constructed personal testimony. That testimony should first clearly outline why we must be saved (delivered from an eternity of separation from God). It should also include God's great love for us that allows us to receive what we could not obtain any other way—except through the acceptance of His Son as Lord and Savior of our lives. In addition, it should explain that it is the power of God's Holy Spirit that draws people to God and keeps us in that relationship with Him forever.

What other elements should you include in your testimony to make it personal? As you progress through your testimony, share specific incidences through which God has guided you, strengthened you and given your life purpose. Also, be prepared to lead whoever you are interacting with to a decision for Christ, and then pray with him or her to accept God's offer of salvation. Encourage that person to allow God to take charge of all of his or her life from this point forward. Making your testimony personal adds validity and credibility to God's invitation, since it is presented by you. All of your words are reinforced by the display of these truths as you live them out in your own life every day.

After you live your life in a Christ like manner, share your testimony and garner a firm commitment from another person to Christ, your next step to fulfill God's General Order is dedicating yourself to disciple the new convert. You teach them how to "be" what they have just become. That multiplication process is how a single-minded Christian soldier obeys the General Order of "going and teaching."

Why does God choose to involve believers in the plan of salvation for others? Honestly, I'm not 100% clear on that. Personally, I would not trust us with that serious mission. But, the bottom line is, that's what He decided to do.

I do not understand why God does a lot of things He does. However, this I do know: **my understanding is not a prerequisite of my obedience.** So, we should accept that we are expected to be active in doing God's will. As single-minded soldiers, taking others along for the ride is our key marching order and part of our job description.

The Bible often requires us to use "child-like faith" to believe in God. Wouldn't it make sense that we obey our marching orders with child-like obedience? I think many of our experiences with God mirrors our experiences with our earthly parents. My Mom's generic, bottom line answer to my question, "Why?" was always and quite simply: *"Because I said so."*

My lack of understanding was not justification for me not to fulfill my responsibilities as her child. I was hers and she had the right to bless me or to spank me. Can you see how much more important it is to obey God's instructions, as our Heavenly Father? He has the same rights on a much larger scale! Sometimes we will not understand His ways but we must obey Him and do what He says simply because He is God and He said so.

Many times in the Bible we are commanded to "search Him," "know Him" and to "go" and "do." These are not just good suggestions, they are additional orders!

I learned very quickly as a child of a military officer and then as a soldier myself, that orders are to be carried out—period! I also learned in the military about the different kinds of orders: basic orders and General Orders. Basic orders vary for different objectives and they can change or be modified as the circumstances change and/or options become available.

But General Orders are different. The General Orders are the highest kind of order you can be given—no exceptions, no excuses, no changes, no options and no discussion. I believe that personal evangelism is a holy General Order for every child of God—no exceptions!

How important is it to obey a General Order? It is so important that one of the General Orders is to report any basic order that is contrary to a General Order!

A General Order supersedes any other order! A soldier must not follow any other order that is contrary to it. If he receives such an order, he has a responsibility to report the superior who gave such an order. This example is the only way to actually get in trouble for being obedient to orders.

But let's step away from the military context for a moment to remember that what we are concerned with is spiritual matters. You are to be concerned with the possibility that people you have come in contact with could be "left behind" because **you** didn't do your job.

Your responsibility is to share the Gospel with those people that God brings across your path—no exceptions. It took me a while to realize not everyone has a magnetic, outgoing, confident, approachable personality and that those types may have difficulty sharing the Gospel with others.

Some people, in fact, may be naturally shy. They may not even be able to think about witnessing to someone face-to-face without hyperventilating. But, God's General Order commands us to stop thinking in human terms and get "ourselves" out of the picture.

Personal evangelism is not about you. Nor is it about your talents or abilities—or your lack of them. **Personal Evangelism is about receiving a General Order and obeying it without hesitation.** We must settle this fact in our minds and become firmly committed to obey—period. Words, courage and confidence will all come from God by the power of His Spirit.

Don't let Satan entice you to delay by studying the General Order and by making sure it conforms to your idea of a perfect solution. We are not allowed to modify the implementation or timing of an order. Like the Nike tagline, we are called to "JUST DO IT!"

Once you understand how a General Order works, you won't mind receiving it. You see, there is a truly amazing fact about this General order. You are not responsible for the outcome! Therefore, you have nothing to lose by obeying them!

The results are the responsibility of the commander who gave the order. In the military, if you obey an order and your situation ends up a mess, you are not responsible for the mess. You are a good single-minded soldier that did your duty and obeyed the command…you are off the hook for the outcome!

If we obey God's "General Orders," we provide a platform for the Holy Spirit to accomplish a work of grace in the life of another human being. And, in the process of our obedience, we may receive a heavenly by-product: a blessing. That blessing has nothing to do with our talents and/or abilities. It has everything to do with our obedience to the orders that we have received and obeyed.

As mentioned at the beginning of this chapter, Jesus left us His version of a General Order to make disciples just when he went to Heaven: *"Go ye therefore, and teach…"* (Mathew 28:19, KJV). It was not, sit ye and write ye books or, play ye and sing ye a song. These tools can be very effective supplements, but make no mistake: **there is no substitute for personal evangelism!** It says, "Go YE" and "YE"…is you!

Personal evangelism is a one-on-one, in your face (gently, with love and compassion, of course), Spirit-motivated, Spirt-controlled and Spirit-empowered obedience to the General Order to do your job of making disciples!

Since this order is one of the highest magnitude, let me unpack the qualities you are to possess as you carry out your mission. You are to be:

Spirit-motivated, which means you do what you are told when you are told to do it. You are not early and you are not late. You must always be ready and prepared.

Spirit-controlled, which means you do not push forward or pull back. You allow God's Spirit to work the plan. Just be open to Him changing His leading, and follow it along the path.

Spirit-empowered, which means you do not have the power to save anyone. You are an instrument of God in helping others to become saved. But the power comes from and through His Holy Spirit.

If you do not obey the General Order of making disciples, you are in danger of preempting the perfect plan that God has for your life; you are also affecting the life and the eternal destination of the individual whom you are supposed to reach.

We can only pray that God has other soldiers ready to obey. And, we hope that time will allow them to carry out the order that we have disobeyed so that we don't lose the battle for that person's eternal soul.

Satan's first choice is to get you to directly disobey the General Order of making disciples, but a good single-minded Christian soldier will not select that option. If you consider modifying the General Order in any way, you give the Devil the next best option. (You will also see me refer to this compromising strategy again in another chapter).

"If the Devil cannot get you to blatantly do the <u>wrong</u> thing, he will try to get you to do the <u>right</u> thing, the wrong way, at the wrong time."

This altering of an order midstream is what a good friend of mine calls: "getting ahead of the dogs." I asked him what that meant and he said, *"When you're hunting, you got to make sure you don't get ahead of the dogs, or you could get shot!"*

In case you are not a hunter (or from the South), I'll explain this hunting tip: For the safety of everyone in the hunting party, it is critical that they stay behind the dogs. The dogs are leading the search for the game. If you get in front of them, you could be mistaken for the game and end up with a bullet right in your mistaken position.

If you believe that God is who He says He is—and if you

believe He can do what He says He can do—then let God lead and follow Him with confidence. Do not be afraid for your safety or doubt your success because in God's perfect will—there are no failures!

Complete obedience and absolute allegiance to the Great Commission—our General Order—must be followed to the letter. Otherwise, only a shadow of the Gospel will be presented. Unfortunately, this mistake could cause someone to become a casualty and be…left out!

11.

Spiritually Blindsided

Strengthening Strategy:
Being aware of the potential of friendly fire.

We have already discussed The Great Commission from the standpoint of "go," but the second part of that verse instructs us to "make disciples" (Matthew 28:19, NKJV).

I believe that one of the most neglected aspects of church responsibility today is the discipleship of the "newbies," (short for "new babies" in Christ), otherwise known as new Christians, new converts or new believers.

We bring them into the family, shake their hands and wish them well, hoping they hang on long enough to get to the Promised Land. In the meantime, we both go on our merry way.

A year later, we hear people say things like: *"What ever happened to Bob and Mary? I haven't seen them in months. Maybe they weren't really saved?"*

The problem may be that many "newbies" fall victim to incomplete training, shadows of truth, juicing of the Gospel or what I call being "spiritually blindsided." In the military they call it being a casualty of "friendly fire" or getting accidentally shot by one of their own, not by the enemy.

Even seasoned Christians may have good intentions, but if they are confused themselves about what the full Gospel is and isn't, how can we expect them to train others? How can they tell the "newbies" about how they should and should not act?

It may be purely accidental that the lack of proper discipleship is the reason we have casualties in our own ranks. However, sometimes these casualties are not accidental.

We likely know all too well that there are cases when a fellow believer intentionally wounds another. The reasons range from neglect and/or ignorance of the Word of God, to jealousy, envy and selfish apathy. The bottom line is that newbies—and even some veterans— become utterly confused and discouraged because they feel blindsided. The result? They withdraw. In some extreme cases, they just quit the Christian mission all together.

A pastor, (gee who could that be...?), gave an excellent example of how sudden and destructive being blindsided can be. In one of his sermons, the pastor told the story of a young, good looking and very talented high school football player, who was determined to make it as a professional. The high school player practiced hard and seemed to have what it took to be successful. However, a single occurrence almost ended his entire football career.

He was defensive back and his job was simple: tackle the runner, or, if tackling wasn't possible, make absolutely sure that the runner didn't get around him. His job was to turn the play inward, toward the center of the field and toward his teammates, so that they could help stop the run.

On a very important down, at a critical time near the end of the game, the ball carrier broke through the defensive line and came directly toward this defensive back, who was the only person between the ball carrier and a touchdown. A touchdown would win the game for the other team, so the defensive back knew he had to stop the ball carrier, no matter what.

The defensive back ran toward the ball carrier as fast as he could, fully committed to hit him with every bit of strength that he had. He was totally and intently focused on the runner's legs in hopes of anticipating the slightest change in direction or speed.

He was so focused that, less than one second prior to the impending collision with the ball carrier, a perfectly timed block from the ball-carrier's team mate blindsided the defensive back and rendered him almost unconsciousness.

The impact was so hard that the defensive back's helmet came off. (For a moment, everyone thought his head might still be in it.) He barely remembered the crowd rising to their feet and applauding his valiant effort as they carried him off the field.

After the game, the coach remarked, *"Son, that was one of the hardest blocks I have ever seen! Are you sure you are OK?"* It would be days before the player totally recovered from something he never even saw coming.

The defensive back was right where he needed to be to make the play. He was focused and ready to do his job. In fact, he was so focused on hitting the runner, that he didn't have a clue about what was about to hit him.

Some wise person said, *"As long as you live, you will have problems. You are either coming out of a problem, you are currently in a problem or you are headed toward a problem. Fortunately for us, many problems provide some notice, but others just totally blindside us."*

As church members and Christian co-workers acting as single-minded soldiers, we can plan, prepare and concentrate on solving problems and doing our jobs. We even get pretty good at anticipating problems and dealing with them in advance. We may also be in the right place, properly equipped and totally dedicated to do our job—when all of a sudden—WHAM! We get blindsided by someone or something that we never expected.

What is even worse...is that sometimes we are blindsided by someone who we know, trust, respect or even love. The surprise "whack" may be from a co-worker, a relative or a fellow church member.

I am not suggesting that this intentional whacking is an epidemic in our churches, but it does happen too frequently. Salvation makes us perfect once we arrive in Heaven. In the meantime however, we are all susceptible to making mistakes and blindsiding someone or being blindsided by someone else.

If we can recognize the symptoms of someone who is in the beginning phase of thoughtlessly wounding a brother or sister in the body of Christ, we may be able to stop the problem dead in its tracks. Perhaps then we will see fewer of our sisters and brothers crushed, discouraged, broken and blindsided.

Some people in churches may blindside others by doing what they truly believe is right. They appoint themselves judges and jury members for all that goes on in "their" church. We will look at them more closely in the next chapter.

Paul tells us the responsibility of what we do as Christians lie with us. *"One man esteems one day as better than the other, while another man esteems all days alike (sacred). Let everyone be fully convinced (satisfied) in his own mind"* (Romans 14:5, AMPC). So, we must not allow ourselves to be used for wrong-doing or influenced by it.

The King James Version says it this way: *"One man esteemeth one day above another, another esteemeth every day alike. Let every man be fully prepared in **his own mind**"* (Romans 14:5, KJV, bold emphasis from this author). No matter how you translate this verse, we are responsible for our own actions.

Just a moment, though, fearless leader! Don't jump out there and say that this verse means that you can make your own decision about what is right and wrong. Or, just in case you think that no one can tell you what to do, let's examine this biblical principle a little closer.

First, look at the words, "your own." Paul reminds us: *"You are not your own, you have been bought with a price"* (1 Corinthians 6:20, NIV). This verse means that "you" are not in charge. You—and your old fleshly ways—are actually supposed to be dead! Your flesh is to be crucified with Christ. Therefore, you do not make decisions! Christ makes them—and you obey. But, when and if you are disobedient, you ARE responsible for the wrong decisions that you make.

Second, what should we think about our minds? Well, when you tell your friends that you got saved, they will usually say: *"You've lost your mind!"* Your response should be: *"Oh, thank you for that positive reinforcement! I now know I made the right decision."*

In fact, we are instructed **not** to have the mind that we used to have, but because we are saved, we should have the mind of Christ. *"Let this mind be in you, which is also in Christ Jesus"* (Phil 2:5, KJV).

The Amplified Classic version of 1 Corinthians 2:18–19 also describes the pursuit of a Christ-like mind:

"But the spiritual man tries all things (he examines, investigates, inquires into, questions, and discerns all things), yet is himself to be put on trial and judged by no one (he can read the meaning of everything, but no one can properly discern or appraise or get an insight in him. For who has known or understood the mind (counsels and purposes) of the Lord so as to guide and instruct Him and give Him knowledge? **But we have the mind of Christ** *(the Messiah) and do hold the thoughts (feelings and purposes) of His Heart."*

The same verses in the King James Version says it a little differently: *"But he that is spiritual judgeth all things, yet he himself is judged of no man. For who hath known the mind of the Lord, that he may instruct him?* **But we have the mind of Christ"** (1 Corinthians 2:18–19, KJV). (In both versions, I have added bold for emphasis.)

No matter what translation you use, the message is the same. You are instructed to use the "mind of Christ" that has taken up residence in you. You are not to use your human brain that used to be in charge, but rather, you are to use the new mind that you are in the process of developing through obedience to God's Word.

As you develop the mind of Christ, it is Christ who will teach you, guide you and give you insights about his purpose for you. And when you allow Him to do that, NO ONE can judge what you do. Or, they would be judging Christ, who is judged by no one. Christ is the true substance and He cannot be judged. He is not a shadow that can be defined differently by each person as they choose to see Him.

Your pastor/teacher and other seasoned Christians will also play a role in your Christian development, provided that they are focused on the substance rather than the shadows. But the responsibility to ultimately be led by Christ is up to the individual believer.

If we are not careful, we will settle for a convenient religious shadow *of* Christ rather than a personal relationship of substance *with* Christ. This mistake could become a reality if we do not pursue the mind of Christ who was himself, the Ultimate Single-Minded Soldier and the One that we are called to pattern our minds after. His mind is protection for us and it helps to keep us from being used to blindside others. Christ's mind working in us keeps us from knocking others…out of the game.

12.
"So Butch Says to Sundance..."

Strengthening Strategy:
Identifying and dealing with the relentless pursuit of human judgment.

The movie, *Butch Cassidy and the Sundance Kid* is a great film. I have watched it several times. It was so well done that when you watch it, you actually end up rooting for the bad guys to win! At the very least, you want them to survive. You may not see the connection to growing as a single-minded Christian soldier, yet, but I promise, it's coming...hang tight.

The movie was a magnificent combination of romance, action, history and intrigue with some really great one-liners. The plot depicts two outlaws, Butch Cassidy and the Sundance Kid, who are pursued by the relentless posse of veteran lawmen led by an infamous Indian tracker.

No matter how or what Butch and Sundance did to try to throw the law posse off of their tracks, the relentless efforts of the lawmen kept finding them. Finally Butch Cassidy turns to Sundance and says out of total desperation, *"Who are those guys?"*

In the Bible, some self-appointed "trackers" relentlessly pursue others to hold them accountable to the Law. That is, the Law the way they interpret it to be. The trackers were called Pharisees. They were shadows of what God's chosen people were supposed to be like. They were more concerned with tracking down, judging and convicting others who they thought did not measure up to their version of the law than they were to living the life that they claimed to represent.

Before the Apostle Paul became a Christian, he was the chief bounty hunter. He was a Pharisee tracking down and convicting Christians. He was both a prosecutor and a judge! In fact, he had papers that allowed him to carry out sentences that included the execution of anyone he convicted on the spot!

Christians are God's other chosen people, in addition to the Jews. Because of the gifts that God has given us, we have been given the power to recognize these shadow-focused posse members—like Paul before his conversion. These people claim to know God, the true substance. They point toward the substance, but their focus is misguided. They skew the proportion of the importance of their viewpoint, which is small in comparison to salvation issues.

Who are these guys? I'm talking about the "Translation Police," the "Grace Guards," the "Motivation Marshals," the "Clothing Cops," and last but not least, the "Kosher Kings" and "Shadow Czars" that spiritually blindside the newest people in their fellowship with the skill of a true Pharisee.

We are to identify these people, but unlike Paul, we don't want to kill these groups, we just want to get them on the right track or avoid them if necessary!

I'm not making these groups up—they are in the Bible! I just named them a little differently. So let's take a closer look to see if you recognize any of these people. You may have encountered them in your church.

Translation Police: This person or group determines which Bible translation or training literature more closely resembles the language of Heaven. (King James, American Standard or the Original Hebrew and Greek.) Obviously, we should be careful to protect the integrity of God's Word. However, I am equally confident that obedience to the 99% that we do agree with will produce a better and more productive outcome than debating the 1% we disagree on.

Grace Guards: These "guards" believe their job is to certify who is really saved and to determine if they were baptized correctly, etc. They examine every aspect of a Christian's life and from time-to-time, they give "pop quizzes."

Motivation Marshals: They try to determine the real meaning behind your efforts and works. They detect your gifts and talents and even try to read your mind. This group's cheerleading is usually biased as a result of their own motives and they will exert the appropriate amount of pressure at just the right time to win you over to their side.

Clothing Cops: These are the people who classify and categorize appearance and apparel. They say what's "in" and what's "out" for the current spiritual season. From clothes to make-up, hair styles and color to length and quality and fit of garments, they will express their opinions without hesitation. They believe that appropriate garments and appearance are crucial to real worship.

Kosher Kings: These self-appointed royals tell us what we can and cannot do, where we can go or what we can be, according to their interpretation of Scripture. These guys work closely with the "shadow czars" and collaborate on denominational issues, church structure, programs, mission efforts and financial expenditures.

Lastly…Shadow Czars: These administrators are responsible for supervising all of the above, including, but not limited to: keeping the pastor in line and ensuring the entire church stays on track. Relatively unknown to the majority of the members, they usually work in pairs. But, they will not hesitate to enlist the help of any, or all, of the other groups mentioned above.

Where are these groups mentioned in the Bible? Let's take a look at John 9:11–34, and ask the Lord to help us identify these groups. *"Now it was on the Sabbath day that Jesus mixed the mud and opened the man's eyes. So now again the Pharisees asked him how he received his sight. And he said to them,*

'He smeared mud on my eyes, and I washed, and now I see''' (John 9:14–15, AMPC).

In these verses, the Pharisees are acting like the "Kosher Kings" and "Translation Police." They are trying to determine if this activity is a supernatural miracle or just a trick. It did not look "kosher" to them and they did not remember anything in the Torah that would substantiate it.

A little later in the same chapter, it says: *"Then some of the Pharisees said, 'This Man [Jesus] is not from God, because He does not observe the Sabbath'"* (John 9:16, AMPC). Enter the "Grace Guards," who determine He is not of God, but instead they determine that He is a sinner. His sinner status is obvious because he is doing this healing thing on the Sabbath.

Then, the Pharisees asked: *"Is this your son, whom you reported as having been born blind? How then does he see now?"* (John 9:19, AMPC). Here we see the "Motivation Marshals" trying to get to the bottom of this situation. They were wondering what Jesus' motive was for healing this boy on the Sabbath. Let the inquisition begin!

It is interesting that the blind man's own family did not support him, but rather, they thought that the Pharisees already knew the truth. *"But as to how he can now see, we do not know; or who has opened his eyes, we do not know. He is of age. Ask him; let him speak for himself and give his own account of it"* (John 9:21, AMPC). His parents were not willing to go there. It was as if they were saying, *"He can speak...ask him. We don't want to get involved."*

I love this...later on, the young man who received his sight gets a little ticked off with this line of questioning and the Pharisees relentless pursuit of the answer. He then smarts off a bit: *"I do not know whether He is a sinner and wicked or not. But one thing I do know, that whereas I was blind before, now I see"* (John 9:25, AMPC). It was as if he said: *"So, stick that in your Ecclesiastical pipe and smoke it!"* (I just love that word, "ecclesiastical.")

Later, they call in the "Shadow Czars" to drop the hammer. *"So they said to him, what did He [actually] do to you? How did He open your eyes?"*

(John 9:26, AMPC). They wanted the bottom line; they were asking him what happened so that they could judge the action.

In an attempt to pin the blind man down and trip him up, the Pharisees "revile" him and tell him that he is a sinner because he collaborates with the sinner who performed the miracle on the Sabbath. Finally, when they have had enough, the self-appointed jury reaches a verdict.

The following verse recounts the discourse of the Pharisees: *"They retorted, 'You were wholly born in sin [from head to foot]; and do you [presume to] teach us?' So they cast him out [threw him clear outside the synagogue]"* (John 9:34b, AMPC).

The Pharisees' message here is very clear. If we can't control them, we will get rid of them. We will do whatever it takes to keep our shadows intact.

The Pharisees' purpose is equally clear. Keep religious activity intact. Maintain it according to what they are comfortable with and can explain in human terms. If anything new or unexplained pops up, immediately label it as evil. Extinguish it quickly and be prepared to do whatever it takes to keep the Pharisee-approved order and control.

When shadows become a satisfactory substitute for substance, our next generation of disciples will be doomed to stay right there...in the shadows.

Another part of our job as single-minded soldiers is to fight the noise and ruckus stirred up by these previously mentioned "authorities." We must seek our one true Single-minded Soldier, Jesus Christ, and test the laws that are put forth by various "religious" people to see if their words line up with the totality of Scripture. Doing so will enable us to keep shining Christ's light to the lost world, rather than staying hidden...in the shadows.

13.
Rapture or Rupture?

Strengthening Strategy:
Addressing this highly controversial topic that could split a church.

The mysterious catching away of believers known as "The Rapture" has always been a difficult concept both to grasp and explain. Some things God just leaves as a mystery. However, as single-minded soldiers, He still calls us to trust Him and believe His Word. Throughout His Word, He promises that He will guide us through the tough times.

He also tells us to seek unity with other believers, and to not let the matters that we don't fully understand divide us. In some instances, the topic of the Rapture has caused division, or a "rupture" in the church. Some churches have even split and pastors have been fired because of their position on this single subject.

Some pastors have chosen not to get specific on this potentially volatile topic. Or, even worse, they have chosen not to address it at all.

Many theories swirl around about how we may be living out end-time prophesies. Some believe that the Rapture will take place before the tribulation time prior to Christ's second coming (pre-trib). Some believe it will happen in the middle (ah-trib) while others believe it will happen at the end of the tribulation period (post-trib). People have been debating these theories for hundreds of years, and we aren't going to solve them here.

"Pre-millennial," "ah-millennial" and "post-millennial" philosophies are also thrown into the mix. Well, we are not going to debate those in this book either.

I like my father-in-law's thoughts on the matter. He said, *"I prefer the 'pan theory.' There is a lot of controversy on just where we are in history, but if your personal relationship with God is right, and focused on God's will for your life, it will all 'pan out' in the end."*

Some preachers are not easy to pin down on their position. They are neither "pre-," "ah-" or "post" anything. They are simply "NGT (Not Going There)" because it is too controversial.

Others shy away from the topic because of the time that it takes to thoroughly research and prepare to teach this complex subject. Still others find it simpler and safer to find an ETS (End-Times Specialist), who will come in and do a week-long seminar with a section on the Rapture.

If you think about it, hiring an ETS is really a good idea! This specialist comes in, shares his opinions and leaves. The pastor, who has to stay, also benefits in several ways:

First, he satisfies the curiosity surrounding end-time events for his flock (and probably for himself).

Second, he maintains a safe distance from a difficult, volatile and potentially career-changing event.

No matter what your position is on this controversial topic called the Rapture, the bottom line message is always the same—some are taken away and others are left behind.

Therefore, it makes sense that something has to be the cause of many people being left behind. Otherwise, they would not really be left behind at all. (You might need to read that again, slowly.)

We cannot shrug off people being left behind as simply a result of their own foolish choices and take the position that it is simply not our responsibility. That attitude displays a considerable amount of ignorance about what God calls us to do as part of our Christian service. It also displays selfish motivations and shows that your level of care for others, including concert about important life and death issues, has left the building.

Some Christians have left out important things in their

testimony, modified other parts and simply ignored some issues altogether. Others have learned how to "spin" everything to suit their needs. This distortion of the truth will cause confusion at best.

We must remember that we are going to be held individually responsible for what we preach, teach and share, and we are going to be held accountable by God for how we live. God will require an answer for every opportunity that we have missed, shied away from or flat out ignored. So we must stay focused and ensure that our motives are crystal clear and in line with the teachings of Jesus. We must remember our mission as single-minded Christian soldiers to *"go and make disciples."* And, we must act on every occasion.

Only then, when we remain steady and ready to carry out our orders for Jesus, our Supreme Commander, can we be certain that everyone we have come in contact with, will have the opportunity to choose...not to be left out when the time does come.

14.
CSI Evangelism

Strengthening Strategy:
Examining the evidence in Christians' lives so that non-believers know the truth.

OK, I admit it. I am hooked on the television series, CSI (Crime Scene Investigation). I love analyzing facts and coming up with the truth— and I advocate that process for anyone serious about becoming a stronger single-minded Christian soldier.

CSI, which is slated to end in late 2016, has maintained some of the highest TV ratings ever. It commands stellar audience reviews even after 15 years of murder, guts, blood, hacking, slicing, choking, shooting and testing.

Even the re-runs hold some of the highest ratings among all television programs ever, (except MASH, which is another one of my favorite shows)!

The series is based on getting to the truth through scientific testing and careful examination of the evidence that was left behind at the crime scene.

The series began in Las Vegas, also known as Sin City—what an appropriate name for that place! In the early CSI episodes, we were first introduced to the significance of bugs, flies and beetles. Then came the difference between spatter and droplets, and the fact that the nearest thing to a dead human was a dead pig.

The next CSI series was filmed in Miami. This series features an actor who always stands sideways and looks up at you (no matter how short you are), puts on his sunglasses and says something really provocative and awe-inspiring at the beginning of the program like, *"It's what we do."* Wow! Is that deep or what?

The female agents all wear Prada, and they gather slime from the swamp in white lab coats and high heels—and yet, they never break one French-manicured fingernail in the process.

CSI New York came along next and gave us a reprieve from a corny lead character. It brought us to the other end of the spectrum, though, with Mr. Super-Serious, Stone Face. This guy has never heard a funny joke in his life. I watch him and say, chill dude! Lighten up a bit and enjoy life!

Then, the show morphed into my personal favorite, NCIS (Naval Criminal Investigative Service)! Yeah! Let's give it up for Gibbs and Denoso! (I love the part when Denoso gets a slap in the back of the head from the boss as a reality check.)

In addition to the various versions of CSI, many other programs investigate the absolute truth by close examination of the evidence, which leaves nothing out of the equation. Another one of my favorite shows is *Cold Case*—you should check it out sometime.

I heard they were going to do a CSI Washington DC, but they couldn't find a story with a truthful ending. All the evidence was too well hidden and they couldn't possibly arrest all the guilty parties because no one would be left to do the second episode. Now that's funny! And that fact hits the nail on the head if you think about the climate in Washington…but I digress.

Isn't it amazing how God can teach us through any means he chooses? Even secular television affirms that if you research enough evidence, you will always get the truth. These programs make it clear that you cannot simply glance at the superficial evidence based on logical assumptions, past experience and/or educated guesswork and arrive at an accurate conclusion. The only way to get to the truth is to collect, test and carefully examine all the evidence—before you share your findings and make a final decision.

Although CSI often featured some really good investigators, the church today seems to be filled with another type of CSI agent.

Unlike thorough investigators, these CSI agents are woefully unprepared for the task of researching and finding the truth. They are Christians that are Spiritually Ill-equipped.

These agents are either uneducated, unqualified or perhaps even unwilling to fulfill the previously mentioned Great Commission to make disciples.

Let's be honest. If we are going to address the problem about what has been left behind in Christianity, we must first admit and accept that the problems lie with people. The problems are with God's people, and the problems are personal.

Each one of us must examine our own hearts and ask God if we lack motivation and/or training. Then, it is our job to become equipped by seeking help. Many times, we can become prepared for discipleship by enrolling in a Bible study of some type at our church.

If you don't like to be around people, don't use that as an excuse. You can also learn to be a disciple and gain skills online through daily Bible study, reading blogs from trusted biblical sources or joining online Christian communities. You can also find a video-based Bible study at a Christian Book Store or at an online book store that will pique your interest.

It is also the believers' responsibility to personally evangelize (or share our faith). We must also realize that it is **not** the responsibility of non-believers to be inquisitive. They are not going to be motivated to gather, collect, test and carefully examine all the evidence in the Bible in an attempt to determine where they stand in relation to God. They won't do that simply because they don't see the need—or they simply don't care!

However, one of the things that can generate curiosity is difference. God calls us to be a "peculiar people." [*"But ye are a chosen generation, a royal priesthood, an holy nation, a peculiar people"* (1 Peter 2:9, KJV.)]

Unfortunately, when non-believers look at Christians today, they don't see much of a difference between us and them. Many of those who are "peculiar" are just peculiarly weird. Therefore, many non-believers do not see an incentive to change or investigate at all.

God wants us to demonstrate a peculiarity that causes others to have genuine interest. He wants our lives to entice others to find out why we are different. He wants them to be intrigued enough to think that something about us is worthy of further investigation.

I believe one of the best confirmations that a Christian can receive is when someone says, *"There is something different about you. What is it?"* Or, *"I can't quite put my finger on it, but there is something about the way you talk or act that is different."*

This sense of intrigue that people discover about you suddenly entices them in some way. Perhaps it's because the experience is somewhat like our first romantic encounter. The mystique or the uncertainty—and perhaps to a lesser degree—surprise or apprehension, encourages them to look further. There seems to be a curiosity that demands further discovery.

If we live, act and speak as a representative of God, it will invite discovery. Therefore, every aspect of our life should be open and on display for all to see. It should entice people to thoroughly investigate the reason for our difference.

People will have a much better opportunity to become saved when they see that the evidence of a life lived for God is never…left undiscovered.

15.

Good Fruit or...Wax?

Strengthening Strategy:
Discerning between what is real and what is counterfeit.

One of the first commands that God gave Adam and Eve as the first humans was to "be fruitful and multiply." (I used to think that this saying meant that the punishment for sinning was that you would have lots of fruity children.)

But really, "fruitful" means "like kind and quality." God was actually saying, in my paraphrased interpretation, of course: "Reproduce what *you are* now! I want you to birth and raise up more God-like offspring." That's part of our mission as single-minded Christian soldiers!

Raising up God-like offspring is not an automatic by-product of being saved and joining the church. Making disciples takes time, education, research, examination, perseverance, experience, lots of practice and personal commitment.

If evangelism is not implemented correctly, people may seek only the first part of salvation which is the "escape part" of grace. That's the part that saves them from Hell. But that first part stops short of helping newly saved people understand that they have a job to do on earth once they are saved.

Once people think they are inside Heaven's door, they may want to sit down and coast in their new idea of eternal comfort. But that concept of being saved is only a "shadow" of what abundant life truly is. Sadly, sometimes professed newbie converts continue on with their lives just as they were before with no evidence of any significant change. Many times there is neither change nor fruit; if there is anything, it is, at best, imitation, wax fruit. When real change into Christ-like character occurs, however, real fruit is produced.

If we are not careful, there is another CSI concept that may pop up called **C**hurch-member **S**ubstitutionary **I**nvolvement. That's when we shirk our personal responsibility and hire it done or encourage others to do it for us.

No substitute replaces rock solid, tested and tried personal experience. Without it, we end up with emotional fluff that has no substance. Emotion is not good fruit. It resembles fruit, but it is not the good fruit that God wants and demands.

By the way, have you ever seen a bowl of fake fruit on someone's table? I've always thought, *"That's cruel...What's the point of that?"* Be honest. Have you ever picked up fruit in a bowl to see if it was real or not? Many people cannot tell by looking if the fruit in question is an imitation or the real thing. I'm an advocate for banning wax fruit—it's just not right.

Please don't misunderstand me. I'm not saying that emotion should be eliminated. I believe that emotion plays a very important part in worship. In fact, I am a very emotional person. (I get emotional just reading what I have written up to this point...so excuse me a moment.) OK, I'm back. But, *emotion should be a by-product of an act of worship, not a catalyst to try and launch it.*

Emotion cannot be a satisfactory substitute either! Emotion without experiential knowledge, commitment and the right motive is at best, a "flesh" in the pan. [Get it, a f-l-e-s-h in the pan—(instead of flash in the pan)?] Now that's funny!

Now, go back and read the previous paragraph again and enjoy some truly great humor and yes, you have my permission to use it. (See, I told you if you have to explain humor...it loses something.)

The term "flesh" is used in the Bible to refer to things that are not spiritual. These things are human or world-like. The flesh can refer to anything in our bodies that may temporarily satisfy our desire for physical love or acceptance. The term "flesh" can also encompass various emotions like power, pride, anger, selfishness, greed, lust and much more.

Once we are saved, our flesh becomes our enemy. We know there is a better way, and yet, we still struggle against these human traits.

God doesn't want us to be consumed by the "flesh," so what is He seeking from us instead? How does He enable us to live victoriously in spite of these struggles? By His Spirit. God commands us to be students of the Word. He is after the daily readers, the inquiring minds, and the committed and diligent truth seekers, who witness boldly based on knowledge and understanding. He seeks defenders of the faith. He longs for us to develop into courageous warriors willing to sacrifice themselves for the cause of Christ. That journey as a single-minded soldier requires us to have a Christ-mind, not an emotionally-driven flesh response.

After we are saved and have experienced a supernatural event, He wants our lives to be permanently affected by that encounter. He wants us to let the miracle transform the very fabric of our lives. When either another believer or a non-believer sees a walking miracle, that's something to truly get emotional about.

We find ourselves wondering why our children leave the church once they leave the nest. In many cases, it is because the elements encompassed in "Christianity" as they knew it, were only songs, stories and some emotionally driven enthusiasm. They never truly saw—nor did they personally experience—the supernatural movement of the Spirit of God in their life as a daily staple. Rather, it was an unexpected interruption in their shadow routine.

I am not saying that these young people are not saved because they have not had an "experience" per se. This book is not going to take the time to debate at what split-second someone is actually saved. And, we won't discuss if someone is saved because they "do this" or "do not do this or that." Nor is it this book's purpose to dissect the trigger that determines when salvation is moved from the head to the heart, etc.

What we are concerned with here are the issues for which God's children are responsible once they have made the decision to follow Christ.

If you have never had a personal, supernatural event in your own life, if you have never seen the Spirit move with your own eyes, or if you have never experienced a special anointing or a miracle of healing, there is little evidence for you or the unbeliever to examine!

No dynamic dimension fuels your basic faith and no supernatural substance catapults your efforts to new heights. And, if something spiritual does manage to scratch the surface, there may not be enough spiritual depth to produce "Godly fruit" or even "good fruit."

If we are not careful, the words we use will have no power, the concepts that we present will have no validity, and the suggestions we make will offer no grounds for serious consideration.

Ultimately, we end up with no takers to join us on this great journey to become a single-minded Christian soldier. We may even get depressed and go AWOL (Absent Without Official Leave). Without enough evidence to justify a change of heart and mind, the unsaved person simply sees a bowl of wax fruit with no nourishing value, and he or she chooses to…leave it behind.

16.
"Go Fish!"

Strengthening Strategy:
Casting your nets where the fish are. How, where and when?

I am going to spend a little time sharing some of my vast experience as a fisherman. (Trust me, this won't take long!)

One of the first card games that I learned as a child was, "Go Fish." It gave me a great feeling when my opponent asked for a card I did not have and I could shout out: "Go Fish!"

Jesus was not talking to his opponent, but He was telling His disciples to "draw" and fish again, but in a different way. He said to them, *"Follow me, and I will make you **fishers of men**"* (Matthew 4:19, KJV). (Therefore, fishing is "in the cards," so-to-speak—get it?)

But in all seriousness, one of the main lessons I have learned about fishing is that timing is very important. In some cases, timing is not a factor—it is *the only factor*. You will not catch fish if your timing is off—period.

Some fish feed early in the morning; others feed at night. Some fish surface at a full moon, and others eat only at a particular time of year. If you try to catch fish that like cold water, you will not catch them in shallow waters in August. Cold water fish won't be around, unless you are in the waters of Alaska. I'm not sure what the Southern fish are doing when they go missing in August. Maybe they are in school. (Get it? A school of fish...some of you are really slow).

OK, now back to my point: No matter if we are talking about fishing or life, timing is important. We touched on timing a few chapters ago and said that *"The next best option for Satan when he can't get you to do the absolute wrong thing, is to get you to do the right thing, in the wrong way or at the wrong time."*

We also know that God commands us to "go." But how do we know when the time is right? You can't catch fish when the timing is wrong and you cannot catch men, (so-to-speak) if the timing is off either.

As I explained earlier, salvation was, is and always will be, the responsibility of the Holy Spirit. He does, however, invite us to become involved in the process. When Jesus himself spoke to people about their relationship to the Father, He did it in the power of the Holy Spirit.

When the Lord went back to Heaven, He changed everything by giving us the responsibility and privilege to become involved in the salvation process of others. The one thing that did not change, however, was the origin of the power and authority that makes a person change. That soul responsibility still lies with God's Holy Spirit. You might say, it's His "soul" responsibility. Get it? (That one wasn't funny but catchy!)

We, however, still get to play a part in this work *at the right time.* How then, do we find out when the time is right? Simply stated—we listen!

We have to communicate with Jesus often enough to recognize His voice. We must learn to understand His ways and to totally rely on Him and to trust in Him. It takes practice, practice and more practice in reading and studying His Word. It also takes praying, attending church services and serving whenever God prompts us to do so.

Someone once said, *"Experience keeps us from making mistakes. Well, then, how do you get experience? By making lots of mistakes."* Albert Einstein said: *"Show me someone who doesn't make mistakes, and I will show you someone who isn't doing anything."*

You may make some mistakes trying to recognize and obey instructions from God. But I believe if your heart's desire is to do God's will, even your failures will prove to be a positive experience.

Only God can turn failures into something so positive and transformative.

Other characteristics of the Holy Spirit are important to understand. He does not yell, He does not interrupt and He does not badger his children. He whispers in what the Bible calls "a still small voice." You might say He is a Holy Gentlemen.

He never forces us to do anything: He is gentle. Even when we deserve a good spiritual smack in the head (like the ones Denoso in CSI used to get—I just can't get away from CSI), He does not act that way. He is patient and kind. He does have His limits and His corrections can be rough, but that method is not his preference. He would rather have you so attentive that you pick up on the slightest nudge, whisper or tingle that you may sense.

Sure, you can fish at the wrong time and even snag a fish or someone's soul for Christ every once in a while solely because God's Word is faithful to itself in spite of your timing and mediocre efforts. But, if you receive a word or nudge from God, that's when you can cast your net with confidence because the time is right and you will make a catch.

The last requirement to becoming a good fisherman is often controversial. A good fisherman needs to go to where the fish are. Duh! You can buy all your gear and even get a fishing license at Walmart. You can also buy a fishing boat, but you can't catch fish there! And, you cannot fish for unsaved people inside your Walmart Church either. Get your gear and training at church, but you will need to be obedient to go where the fish are when you are sent out for "catching" people.

I do not know many Christians who frequent a bar or the extra dangerous parts of town to share the Gospel. We become satisfied to throw a net in front of the pulpit and see if a fish will find it. You may not feel comfortable going where the fish are, but more often than not, they won't be coming to you. You will have to launch out to get them.

For a Christian not to go where unsaved people are makes as much sense as a doctor refusing to go to the hospital because it is full of sick people.

But maybe we need another reason to "go fish." How about a biblical "fish story" that explains going somewhere at an unusual or uncomfortable time? In our story, some frustrated fishermen were washing up and putting things away after a long day of fishing with no results when Jesus told them: *"Launch out into the deep and let down your nets for a catch"* (Luke 5:4, NKJV).

The response in verse 5 was something like: *"We have been fishing all night and we got nada, nothing, zip, zero. But, if it* **floats your boat**, *we'll give it a try…"* (That's my loose translation and please, don't miss the humor…I bolded it for those who were not paying attention.)

What made the difference in their efforts? The second time they cast the nets out when Jesus said it was the *right time* to catch fish, and they had gone to where Jesus said the fish were. They obeyed and they caught so many fish that they thought the boat would sink and nets would rip! Obedience with perfect timing is everything.

When the Holy Spirit has drawn someone to a particular point, and He has assigned you to the same spot, at the same time, that is indeed…perfect timing! Don't worry, be fishing. (I think there's song in there somewhere!)

It's also a good idea to have some bait manufacturers to disciple us in witnessing techniques. And, it would be great if we had fishing rod makers show us how to cast to the right places and to provide just the right pole to make sure we don't lose the fish.

We also need boat builders to help us select the right vehicle to get us to the fish. Tackle box suppliers can help provide us options that we may need if the situation changes. And, precision hook designers show us additional witnessing tools that will keep the fish on the line until the Holy Spirit can reel them in. All of these people—and many more—may be involved in your very first cast. And they say fishing is not a team sport!

Imagine if we could see all the events, people and circumstances involved in just one witnessing opportunity. If we could get a glimpse of all that had to happen in your life to get you positioned, it would be amazing. If we could see the hundreds—perhaps thousands—of supporting people that were involved who also had to be waiting for the right time to help, that would be even more incredible. All of those orchestrations don't even include all the details in the life of the person you are witnessing to, just to arrange an introductory conversation. I believe if we knew about all of the steps involved that the enormity of the task would blow our minds!

Now, multiply all of that synchronized effort times a couple million at one time. Then, figure in the options that have to be in position in case someone misses their opportunity. Well, you get the picture. Only God could manage all that—or do that kind of math!

Let's do our part and listen as well-trained single-minded Christian soldiers. If you are tired of all this work…think of the potential consequences of you not performing your mission.

Just consider what would happen if you don't seize an opportunity or if you are just not paying attention to the Spirit of God's direction and that opportunity is lost. Everything we mentioned above—all the people and all the events—have to be rescheduled for another perfect time before the net can be cast again! If you do happen to miss it, you may be the one…left out of that next fishing trip.

17.
Antiquated Progress

Strengthening Strategy:
Recognizing a contradiction in terms…or a sign of the times?

Antiquated progress…there's another oxymoron (an apparent contradiction for those of us who have forgotten what we learned in English class). Some Christians actually believe that God doesn't really speak to us anymore and that supernatural stuff was for years gone by.

NO! NO! A million times—NO! He never changes! *"Jesus Christ is the same yesterday, today and tomorrow"* (Hebrews 13:8, NKJV). How can anything "supernatural" be antiquated? The real problem is that *we are constantly changing although God remains unchanged.*

Humans see change as a good thing. We call it progress. The problem is that we view the attributes of God against the backdrop of our perceived progress and the changes that we have made. The result is that an unchanging God begins to look farther and farther away from our current perception of reality.

He is either to the left or right of our new perspective and sometimes, we even view Him in the "past tense!" That's right, even with our training as single-minded Christian soldiers, if we are not careful, we may classify what God has done supernaturally as only a historical event.

We may begin to view supernatural events as antiquated solutions that do not apply to modern problems. Instead, we should be seeing an unchanging, Holy Spirit-authored template that can—and should be—applied to our current need.

As a result of dismissing God's supernatural power, we have no anchor for today's chaos. Nor do we have the slightest clue of what we will need in the future.

We have brought God down to our level of expectation based on our experiences, our intellect and our ideas. The result is that we never transcend above ourselves to the supernatural comprehension that we need or the level of obedience that God requires.

Please don't miss this point. This shrinking view of God is the biggest contributing factor that renders God's children useless to the Kingdom! It gives preeminence to just a shadow of God and His power. Underestimating the vastness of God makes us prey to a dangerous position in the Enemy's territory.

What we need to do is raise our level of expectations up to meet the perfect requirements of Holy God! Miraculous, holy and supernatural blessings should be basic, normal expectations for every child of God.

These supernatural encounters, my friends, should be every day occurrences to us. How often and when they occur is still up to God in His sovereign plan. However, these supernatural words, images, impressions, healing's and experiences, are supposed to be the rock solid, fundamental foundation of Christian service.

Anything other than a continual, spirit-filled, holy, miraculous life like Jesus had every day is, in heavenly terms, ABNORMAL!

Above, I have put three paragraphs in bold type on purpose. Please read them again and again. When you have done that, read them again. Yes, I believe it is absolutely critical to your spiritual maturity and survival that you understand these points.

If you do not have high expectations, you will be easily satisfied. Your goals will be consistently and quickly met with simplistic shadows. Your Christian life will never be what it could and should be, and you will not be able to maintain the necessary focus or strength.

Search for truth, and you will find the clues. Study the Bible, and you will gain knowledge. Make your request known, and you will receive. Occupy these and other basic promises of God, and these supernatural signs will be a way of life rather than an occasional interruption of a mundane, religious existence

"But as it is written, Eye hath not seen, nor ear heard, neither have entered into the heart of man, the things which God hath prepared for them that love him" (1 Corinthians 2:9, KJV).

To paraphrase: *"You don't have a clue what God has in store and available to you. And it's not just available to you in Heaven, but you can have those blessings—right here on Earth."*

As you may remember, part or The Lord's Prayer, or the model that He gave us to pray states: *"Thy kingdom come, Thy will be done in earth, as it is in heaven"* (Matthew 6:10, KJV).

Again, to paraphrase: *"Our prayer should be that as things are in Heaven, (perfect, wonderful, and a thousand other positive adjectives…), may they be here on Earth as well."*

God is just as interested in your holy success here, as He is ultimately and eternally…up there.

Be obedient to the commands of God and live up to the expectations of God. His message will ring with such clarity that it cannot and will not be ignored or misunderstood.

Friends, relatives and anyone you share the blessed message of hope with, stands a better chance of not being left behind, when they can see a supernatural demonstration lived out regularly in your life. They will compare your experiences to their lives, and they will easily see what they are missing.

Christians have the awesome responsibility to examine all the evidence that Christ himself left behind **FIRST**! Then—and only then—can they make the perfect truth plain to everyone else in word, deed, example, experience and life-style. Wear your experiences like a soldier's uniform, *proudly and routinely,* on display for all to see—every day.

We are commanded to respond to The Great Commission of making disciples with a sense of urgency and serious dedication. With that mindset, our obedience to the call and our preparation to, *"Go ye therefore, and teach all nations"* (Matthew 28:19, KJV) will be so strong that it cannot be silenced.

Then, in simple "child-like faith," the people we witness to may accept Christ's generous offer of salvation with certainty. And, they would want to receive that gift—not because they had to discover the evidence for themselves—but because they are overwhelmed by the supernatural experiences that are evident and obvious in your life. Now that would be real spiritual progress of a true single-minded Christian soldier!

People need to see that salvation delivers them from wrath and judgment that is coming and know that it grants them eternal life in the sweet by-and-by—yes! But, in addition, your testimony assures them that their salvation paves the way to abundant life here in the nasty now-and-now as well. They will only see that abundant life from consistently observing and verifying the supernatural evidence present in your life.

When we live out that evidence in obedience to His command, we fulfill the first part of the command to produce the "good fruit" that we discussed earlier.

Our personal evangelism must flow from a life that displays the evidence that God still produces fruit in the same way that He always has. Though circumstances change, He does not. Real spiritual progress is realized when we trust in, and rely on and cling to, the unchangeable attributes of God.

We can offer no higher act of worship as single-minded Christian soldiers than to transcend ourselves by clinging to our Lord's unchangeable hand that will never...leave us behind or in the shadows!

18.

Let's Make a Deal

Strengthening Strategy:
Engaging in total wealth management.

Ever since I can remember, I have been instructed by my parents to be a good steward of my time, money and efforts. My dad didn't just teach that—he actually lived it out in front of me his entire life.

He demonstrated all the attributes that are to be aspired to in a model single-minded soldier. He had an incredible level of commitment, combined with honesty, integrity, patriotism and a strong work ethic. All of these qualities were motivated and supported by his complete faith and trust in God. I'm going to brag on him a little more.

Shortly after completing the ninth grade, my father joined the Army at age 16. He was a little young, but poverty, hunger and a single parent home were great motivators in those days. He was promoted from private first class directly to second lieutenant, which is almost unheard of.

This kind of promotion was called a "Battle Field Promotion." He earned it in World War II during the landing at Normandy Beach, where he displayed exemplary heroism and leadership skills.

He also served in the Korean War and in Vietnam twice. He received three Purple Hearts for wounds received in action. In fact, he received one Purple Heart in each of those three wars. He had a chest full of other medals that are too numerous to list that included the Vietnamese Medal of Honor.

He was a certified hard hat deep sea diver, a pilot in the Army

Air Corp and an explosive ordnance disposal specialist. He even set most of the explosives for the epic movie, *The Longest Day*.

Along with 24 years of active military service, he also managed to complete high school, graduate from college and go on to receive a master's degree in criminology, a master's degree in music and a doctorate in divinity. He also became the chief nuclear and thermonuclear weapons analyst for the Department of the Army.

A year after he retired, he was reactivated to military service by presidential decree and served four more years of active military service. Only after an additional 15 years of civil service did he retire for the third and last time.

Those achievements may sound amazing, but what is really incredible is that he did all of this while he also served as an active ordained minister of the Gospel. He wasn't a military chaplain, but he was a civilian pastor and church planter in addition to his military service.

Under the direction of the Baptist Missionary to France, Reverend Jack Handcock, my father and several other men started more than 36 English speaking churches in Europe in less than three years!

At the same time, he also pastored one church full time, located 90 miles south of where we lived for more than a year. Then he served at another church that was 120 miles northeast of our home for almost another year. AND, we never missed a Sunday!

We attended every Sunday morning and stayed for Sunday night service. We even managed to make most of the Wednesday night services as well. We put more than 120,000 miles on that 1959 Ford Station Wagon in two-and-a-half years!

When he finally retired to civilian life, he became a full-time pastor, teacher and church planter until he died in 1992. Busy, busy, busy! I do not ever remember my father just lying around doing nothing. In fact, I don't remember seeing him take a nap! He was up after I went to bed and was gone for work when I got up for school.

He played every brass instrument and did his own auto maintenance and auto body repairs. He was a genius by anyone's measuring stick. In fact, he was often criticized for having a resumé that was more than 20 pages long!

I know what you are thinking: *"Well, what happened to you?"*

I was depressed about that question for a while, but I heard someone say that a genius mentality skips a generation. It was then that I realized it is not my fault that I didn't get any of that genius. It was God's will for my life. I was just like the Apostle Paul, simply "born out of time."

You may ask, how in the world could anyone find the time to do all that? Well, the last time I looked, watches and clocks still have the same numbers on them as they did when my father was alive and you can't make time. You just work hard to fill it.

We can't all be geniuses. But, we all could do better managing our time and selecting priorities. Someone recently said, *"This is the first time in the history of the world that time is now more valuable than money. Because if you only had the time, you could make more money."*

So, what is the problem? The issue is that our priorities have gotten out of whack! Where is the drive not to settle for less? What happened to our level of commitment? Why has God and church taken a backseat to almost everything and where is our desire to excel at something other than our own selfish interests?

To think of stewardship as simply being good money managers is like saying marriage is just two people being friendly on a regular basis.

To understand stewardship on a spiritual level is what the financial world calls "total asset management." Stewardship is more than just throwing our loose change in the plate or punching our spiritual time card once or twice a week at church.

We have developed this strange concept that God was the one that got a great deal because we accepted His offer of salvation. We think He should be satisfied with the time we manage to set aside for Him in our busy schedules. After all, in this day and age, the pressure of everyday life is more demanding than ever. Certainly God knows that.

I was once told that a good deal *"has to be good for both parties, or it is not a good deal."*

God came up with the terms of the good deal of salvation. However, many of us do not keep our part of the bargain; so, it is not such a good deal for God.

We expect Him to keep His part of the deal, which is saving us from Hell. But, when it comes to obedience and living our lives for him, we fall short. Stewardship is based on obedience. It is obedience that is a result of a loving gesture and a desire to obey—it is not simply yielding to an oppressive decree. Nonetheless, being a good steward is a command and part of the salvation agreement.

If stewardship is mostly obedience, what qualifies as obedience? Giving money, time, activity, thought, prayers or service? Stewardship, as I mentioned, is total Christian asset management. The asset we need to manage is our life itself—including every aspect of it! Our lives include those activities listed above and many more.

A good synonym for stewardship is total commitment. Everything I have and everything I am is totally, unreservedly given to God. Giving our lives with unwavering dedication and excellence are key attributes of effective stewardship and being obedient single-minded soldiers.

We cannot allow the pressures of life, the stress of finances and a thousand other things to distract us from our mission or our position. These distractions cannot be given priority over our commitment of stewardship. Our part of the agreement of salvation is to live for him and not ourselves. If we fail to keep our end of the bargain, it's not a good deal. In fact, it's barely a shadow of a deal and the blessings we should and could have, will be…left out.

19.
The Enemy of the Church?

Strengthening Strategy:
Understanding "contemporary praise and worship."

During the past 25 years, we have seen a giant transition from "traditional" to "contemporary" forms of worship. Mix in a little "P&W," (short for **P**raise and **W**orship) music, and you have a full-blown religious revolution.

To understand some aspects about this relatively new concept, we need to peel this onion a bit, unpack a bag and get a clean sheet of paper. It's time to ensure our training as single-minded soldiers isn't too short sighted. We will look at P&W first, then we will examine the terms, "contemporary" and "traditional."

To begin, let me ask you a few questions: Can there be praise without worship? Can you worship without praise? Why do we always put these two words together? Should they be separate?

I don't think so. I would compare separating them to walking with one leg, which no single-minded soldier would do if he still had two legs available. If you intentionally try to walk with one leg, the best you can hope for after you take the first step, is to end up on your face.

In my opinion, one of the highest acts of worship you can offer God is to praise Him. And to praise Him is definitely an act of worship.

I believe that praise and worship are two sides of the same coin. Think about it—can you slice anything so thin that there is only one side? (I know a few sandwich shops that are very close to achieving that...) But my opinion is that although they are different, they are absolutely inseparable.

You could not have a left without a right. You cannot have an up unless there is a down. Without a competent understanding that both sides exist, how do you accurately describe one or the other? Try whistling with one lip!

Let me be clear about this: I do not believe praise is the same as worship. Praise should be worshipful, but I do not think worship can only happen while we are praising God.

I believe true Christianity must involve, display and demonstrate both praise and worship. Praise is what God deserves because of who He is, what He does and because of what He promises. Worship is what we offer, not just in church, but in and with, every facet of our lives, because God is worthy of it.

All that we are and all that we do should be a constant and consistent act of worship. And our lives should be a continual act of worship that praises God in every situation, all the time. Praise and worship is a normal function of a spirit-filled life.

Paul said, *"For me to live is Christ"* (Philippians 1:21, KJV). Therefore, my life should be an act of worship that imitates the life that Christ displayed while he was here. Jesus' life was the model and perfect example of a life that demonstrated both praise and worship.

Our lives are, not our own, because we have been *"bought with a price"* (1 Corinthians 6:20, KJV). We are no longer in charge of ourselves. As I mentioned in the last chapter, stewardship is the "total commitment of everything I have and everything I am, to God." So, technically, even our praise and worship is *not our own*. It belongs to God, and it should be orchestrated and empowered by Him—the owner—as we willfully yield ourselves as a vessel of both.

We have even categorized certain styles of music as "praise and worship" music. More often than not, praise and worship music gets a bad rap. Usually the more traditional churchgoers believe that everyone who participates in that type of music needs to be medicated.

Think about these questions...*How could anyone think that music that is about praising and worshiping God could be bad? Why should music that praises God not include contemporary music?*

I suggest that those who are against certain music in the church come down from the ecclesiastical perch, take off their doctrinal pink glasses and give this an honest examination. (Don't you just love that word…"ecclesiastical?")

How could we possibly confine God to just "this" or "that" little box of human understanding or preference? That notion must be offensive to a multifaceted, all-knowing, omnipotent God of the universe.

Yes, there has to be order and some control that requires some discretion. But we must also be careful not to choke out what we are simply not partial to.

Ask yourself the question: Are hymns "praise and worship?" Sure they are! One very familiar hymn declares it like this, *"Praise God from whom all Blessings flow, praise him all creatures here below. Praise Him above ye heavenly hosts, Praise Father, Son and Holy Ghost."*

That's an old, famous Protestant Doxology[1] and it sounds like praise to me! Yet, it is not considered "contemporary music." What about worship songs? Are they contemporary?

The very first words of the more than 500-year old song, *Oh worship the King* are *"O Worship the King, all glorious above. And gratefully sing, His wonderful love."*[2]

Sounds to me like the idea in this song is "worship." There you have it. Hymns of "praise" and "worship." Yet, strangely so, they are not considered "contemporary."

Therefore, "praise and worship" should *not* be a classification relating to a "style" of music. Rather, those terms should be the very substance and motive for all music that truly seeks to both praise and worship God!

"Praise and worship" is not a category either. Remember they are two sides of the same coin. That coin includes a sincere desire motivated by love *for* God combined with a willful act of responsive obedience *to* God. Those two actions, together, express what He deserves and what you are willing to do. The combination is poetry and/or prose set to music that should include a healthy and accurate balance of both praise and worship.

Now, let's look closely at the other part of that controversy, which has to do with the word "contemporary." When most of us think of a specific word, our mind selects a picture rather than letters or a definition.

Here is an example of how your mind gets a whole picture rather than a partial one. If I say the word "elephant," you see a mental picture of an elephant, not the letters, e-l-e-p-h-a-n-t. I say cow and you see a mental picture of a cow, not the letters c-o-w. But if I say, mother, you probably saw not just a woman but more than likely, you saw a mental picture of *your mother.*

The information we store in our little brain bucket is categorized and then filed according to our understanding and/or our experiences. Sometimes, those categories are generic. Other times they are not. But the categories are always personal based on the decision I made when I set up the file on my mental desktop.

The categories help us retrieve information and make decisions based on our own records. However, the retrieval process can be a problem if instant walls of separation are raised up based on initial faulty information.

When we hear the terms, "praise and worship" or "contemporary," we may become excited because our understanding of these terms happened to be filed in the good drawer of our mental filing cabinet.

On the other hand, those terms may give us cause for concern if a mental sign pops up that says, *"Caution, mind-losing zone!"* or, *"Danger: Wacko's wail and worship here!"*

If we are used to traditional music and we hear contemporary music, our mouth gets dry, our stomach churns and we make finger prints in the pew ahead of us until the service is over and we can get back to "real worship" like…the good old hymns.

Sometimes, perhaps in haste, we process these feelings with a mind-numbing indifference combined with a little starch in our ecclesiastical shorts. (I do love that word…"ecclesiastical," don't you?)

I believe part of our problem is that we don't fully understand the word "contemporary." When you think of that word, it would be more accurate to think of it as "today's music" or "current events."

You may have even heard some people in your own church say: *"The contemporary music that those young people do today is just not right. I don't think God approves of it, I sure don't, it's just…well, ungodly."*

We must understand that the word *"contemporary" is a relative term. It is not a type of music or a stylistic presentation. It is a point in time.* If we say, *"This person is a contemporary of mine,"* that phrase simply means that this person is *currently* living at the same time as I am. It also generally implies that you are currently associated with that person in some way.

The good news for some of you is that "contemporary" is not malignant. What is "contemporary" today will be "traditional" tomorrow and an "oldie" in a few years. "Contemporary" music of today will be fond memories for my grandson when the next generation of "stuff" comes out. (I probably won't think it is music either!)

In short, I encourage those who have issues with "contemporary" or "praise and worship" to get over their issues and use words like "new" and "different." Behold, old people pass away, (meaning you and me) and all music hath become new and contemporary. (Sorry, I cannot pinpoint exactly where that is in the Bible.)

So if you are afraid of the praise and worship music churches are doing now—don't be. Just make sure the music is biblically sound. Also be thankful that people who like this new type of music are in church acting a little strange and not out in the church parking lot slicing the tires on your SUV because what they swallowed or smoked is "contemporary!"

Stagnation can come from not being flexible (within the confines of Scripture). And, when Spirit-filled, Spirit-controlled, creative minds are at work, they will come up with new ways to express both praise and worship to God. These new ways makes praise and worship personal, special and unique to that generation. After all, the Bible says that the opposite of this creativity is called *"vain repetition"* (Matthew 6:7, KJV).

Let's be informed and focused, careful and accurate, sensitive and protective, as all single-minded Christian soldiers are called to be But, we cannot cease to grow in our praise and worship. God is new, every day. That means He is also always contemporary and outside the confines of time. Can we really afford to leave experiencing Him in every possible way behind?

Reference
[1] Trinitarian Doxology, Wikipedia, public domain
[2] Grant, R. (1839). Lyons. 10S and Praise of Divine Love. Retrieved January 12, 2016, from http://biblehub.com/library/lorenz/the_otterbein_hymnal/28_lyons_10s_&_11s.htm

20.

The Dimensions of God

Strengthening Strategy:
Enrolling and completing Supernatural Discovery 101

God loves us. He wants to commune with us and He never gives up on us, even when we are out of line and daily failing at our job. It takes a supernatural mind to understand a supernatural desire and an unwavering, difficult commitment like that. It's a commitment that I can't even begin to understand fully.

What I do know is that when we accept His offer of salvation, it thrills Him. Conversely, when we do not make time for him or elect to do His will, it grieves Him greatly.

If we do not see God with spiritual eyes, we have no awe, mystery or reverence for Him. If we retain only the introductory understanding of God based on our intellect and physical emotions, we only see a shadow of what we should, and could, be. This illusive shadow keeps us from growing and knowing God in the fullness of Himself. It is important for us to recognize the barriers to knowing God more intimately so that we can dodge that blockade. So, let me explain this concept in a little more detail.

When our expectations of God are limited to a human level of understanding, those expectations are viewed against the backdrop of our ability to comprehend, discover, relate and define Him in the physical realm.

Thus, even the anticipation of supernatural events in our lives continues to dwindle. We become disappointed again and again until we do not anticipate—nor do we expect—any supernatural evidence of being a child of God at all. We become spiritually and supernaturally void.

I believe that one of the most terrible things that we can allow to develop in the Christian life is losing the holy awe and healthy respect of God. If the walls of our cold hearts are not torn down, our reverence for God can diminish. If we rely over and over again on familiarity and routine activities (what we see inside the walls of the natural course of life) rather than the expectation of supernatural events, a total spiritual collapse may be just around the corner.

We may say with our mouth that God is the Creator of the Universe. We may even state that He knows everything and He can do anything. On and on we go with our words of confirmation, affirmation and admiration. And yet, we constantly try to contain Him within the parameters of our human understanding.

Bold affirmation combined with self-imposed restrictions at the same time is exactly how a double-minded man thinks.

This process of trying to fit God into our box of comprehension is a basic, natural function of our humanity. Something in us compels us to identify, define and master everything. Our mindset is that we must achieve whatever we set out to do and that success gives our efforts validity. Many times we have to understand something totally before we are even willing to commit to it just a little.

If we rely on this kind of rationale, we reduce God to simply the Creator of the Universe, we classify the Holy Spirit as just the third person of the trinity, and we minimize Jesus as only the Son of God.

Although all of these attributes—in and of themselves—are absolutely correct, they are far from being comprehensive characteristics of our majestic, omnipotent, omnipresent God-head. They are simply shadows of the magnitude of the Supernatural Trinity.

My dad used to ask me… *"How much is a bag of groceries?"* Of course, I quickly responded, *"I have no idea." "Well, obviously!"* he said, *"It depends on what is in the bag."* A bag of paper towels, toilet paper and a box of cereal doesn't cost much. But a bag with steaks, lobster and a five pound bag of pistachios—that's a different story and worth a small fortune!

When you speak of spiritual matters, the same principle of ascribing differing value applies—and that value depends on your understanding of the events. These events can seem superficial, consequential and shallow or they can be overwhelming, inexplicable and totally miraculous!

When we minimize the works of God, we demean deity. Let's call it what it is—blasphemy! We blaspheme (speak irreverently) against God by bringing all that is holy down to our level of understanding. This downgrading of God's works is an insult of the highest order and we don't even recognize or intend it to be that way. Our apathy and ignorance just makes things worse.

When you experience the slightest bit of a holy event in your own life, or if your catch a glimmer of a supernatural occurrence—in even the most elementary fashion—it should permanently change your perspective of God. And that, my friend, is part of a "Supernatural Discovery 101" class of a Spirit-led life.

A song I know helps to launch my spirit toward a supernatural encounter with God every time I hear it. I am encouraged to love Him more and deeper than ever before. I have never read the words nor have I sung this song when my throat did not close up, my eyes blur and the hair on my arms reach toward the heavens. Let the stanzas minister to you as you read them:

"The Love of God"
The love of God is greater far
Than tongue or pen can ever tell;
It goes beyond the highest star,
And reaches to the lowest hell;
The guilty pair, bowed down with care,
God gave His Son to win;
His erring child He reconciled,
And pardoned from his sin.

Refrain:
Oh, love of God, how rich and pure!
How measureless and strong!
It shall forevermore endure—
The saints' and angels' song.

When hoary time shall pass away,
And earthly thrones and kingdoms fall,
When men who here refuse to pray,
On rocks and hills and mountains call,
God's love so sure, shall still endure,
All measureless and strong;
Redeeming grace to Adam's race—
The saints' and angels' song.

(My favorite)
Could we with ink the ocean fill,
And were the skies of parchment made,
Were every stalk on earth a quill,
And every man a scribe by trade;
To write the love of God above
Would drain the ocean dry;
Nor could the scroll contain the whole,
Though stretched from sky to sky.[1]

To add to the amazement that these words generate, it is important to know: Verse three was penciled on the wall of a narrow room in an insane asylum by a man said to have been demented. The profound lines were discovered when they laid him in his coffin.

My prayer is that I become as demented as he was.

Listen, child of God, you must not only grasp the enormity of these words, but you must also take them in. Consume them, feast on them and burn them into your memory. Use them to stretch the intellectual concepts you now have and move the borders of your understanding to infinity.

The magnitude of His greatness and the depth of His love for us is all but lost when we restrict Him to human understanding. When we lose grasp of this awe, our witness is anemic at best. And, the excitement of our testimony becomes flat and ineffective.

Some in the church have substituted holy homage with familiarity. They have exchanged our divine adoption for a convenient acquaintance and the Priesthood of the Saints of God has been reduced to mechanical routine of attendance and menial participation. May God forgive us!

The tendency of humans to reduce God's magnificence remind me of my photographs of Alaska. When I was actually there and witnessed the beauty of Alaska, I was in awe! Unfortunately, the hundreds of photos I took in an attempt to explain what I saw, smelled and experienced, did not even come close to the real thing.

The Bible tells us that *"Eye has not seen, nor ear heard, nor have entered into the heart of man, The things which God has prepared for those who love Him"* (1 Corinthians. 2:9, NKJV).

Many places that I have visited or know about here on Earth make me think, *"This is what it must look like in Heaven."* Then, I remember—THIS EARTH IS CURSED!

When we view deity against the backdrop of the beauty and awe of a "cursed earth," our Heavenly Father begins to come into spiritual focus and Saint of God, that picture is one heavenly ordained Kodak moment.

I encourage you to go back and read the words of the song "The Love of God" again. Let your mind soar, and pull down the limits of logic and familiarity. Widen the possibilities and try to see colors you that have never seen and dimensions that you have never experienced. Let your emotions go higher than ever, and experience excitement and anticipation that is new with every moment. Try and visualize the light that comes from the very throne of God that sheds light on new facets of God continually. God's love is better than all that!

In summary, if we allow ourselves to reduce God to our level of understanding, then the enticing, exciting and mystical awe of Holy God will be reduced to a familiar, faint shadow. But, if we raise our level of expectations up to meet the demands of our Holy God, then we will work, live and dwell as single-minded Christian soldiers in the supernatural. Now—as well as then in Heaven—nothing—I repeat—nothing—will be...left out.

[1] *The Love of God*, Frederick M. Lehman, 1917, public domain.

21.

Sticks and Stones and Broken Bones—But His Words Will Never Harm Me

Strengthening Strategy:
Trusting in what God allows…even though we may not understand it.

As mentioned previously and you have likely observed by now, some chapters in this book are humorous and some are not. This chapter is one that is not so humorous. I just could not find anything funny about "words" and how important the selection, timing and use of words are for the believer.

The ability of our tongue to build up or destroy, can be both a blessing and a curse. An uncontrolled tongue is ungodly and we should firmly stand our ground on that! However, when it comes to practicing the positive selection and use of words, we do not stand quite as firm.

We should take the position that, as bad as the negative use of words are, the demand to select the appropriate good words is even higher. In fact, if we are to overcome evil with good, it makes sense that more focus should be placed on the good words used in our testimony—the testimony we present in both WORD and deed.

If the words of our testimony are to have any power, they must come from a Spirit-controlled heart to our Spirit-controlled tongue. Remember the Scripture we used earlier that confirms this principle? *"O generation of vipers, how can ye, being evil, speak good things?* ***For out of the abundance of the heart the mouth speaketh"*** (Matthew 12:34, KJV). Let me give you one example of words that come from a Spirit-controlled heart. We will again use music as our medium.

I am convinced that many of the words that the hymn writers selected were actually mirrors of the course and purpose of their lives, thoughts and dreams. The lyrics were carefully selected to represent the writer's spiritual encounter, and the hymn became what we might call a collection of "grace occurrences."

Some melodies may reflect eye-witness accounts of supernatural miracles by hundreds or perhaps thousands. Others may describe the love of God that can only come from a single, private, intimate experience.

No matter how big or small the events, and no matter the causes, the inspiring nuggets of truth found in the songs were the result of a supernatural encounter with holiness, set to a heavenly-orchestrated symphony.

These words were placed in the mind and heart of many saints who had looked into the very face of God and stood in awe. They seized the opportunity to translate a heavenly vision into human understanding and recorded it for others to enjoy.

These hymns and songs represent a supernatural revelation that captured the heart and mind of a willing explorer. That revelation guided this spiritual pioneer who had ventured into the unknown in search of his God with lofty and confident expectations of finding Him.

Each revelation of that kind pulls the writer in closer to learn more about Him. The explorer-writer grows to love God even deeper. Then he records his experience by creating a map so that those who follow after him would not lose their way. Rather, others would be encouraged to press on toward their own destinations of worship with confidence.

What is even more amazing is that often the blessed journey was birthed out of agony and/or despair rather than joy or hope. It is the spiritual reality of this blessed event—good or bad—that catches the searcher off guard. He may have had no clue that such a dark time could end in light, peace and joy.

He was likely thinking, *"How could such a negative earthly event have resulted in such a deep, heavenly understanding and meaning? Why am I now so at peace within this pain? How can my mind be so still and confident in the midst of such suffering and chaos? And yet now, what was intended to hurt and destroy, becomes a testimony of faith, encouragement and assurance. Everything was allowed for the greater good."*

The writer's focus becomes redirected away from a negative circumstance as he begins to see the real plan and purpose that God was orchestrating out of the difficult situation. So he answers the divine call to preserve the moment for us. With pen in hand, he translates the language of death and destruction into words of life. Words about "The Word," who was made flesh! One hymn writer said it like this: *"Teach me faith and duty, beautiful words, wonderful words, wonderful words of life, Beautiful words, wonderful words, wonderful words of life."* [1]

As he puts pen to paper, not only do the words come, but they transcend any previous definition or even their former relationship to each other. Where else can you see beauty in words like blood when it is used next to the word atonement? How can suffering be associated with joy? How is serving related to pleasure? How do you comprehend the reversal of words like last being better than first? And how does the least become the greatest?

This metamorphosis can only be as a result of a personal encounter with the Most High God in the Spirit realm. There, God gives us divine interpretation and clarity as we view this message against the backdrop of our misconceptions and presumptions! The hymn writer has obviously been in the presence of the King. He is equally as confident and sure as the eyewitness who stood at the door of the empty tomb and heard the words: *"Why seek ye the living among the dead?"* (Luke 24:5, KJV).

That kind of confidence is the only possible explanation of why the passing of a dying "saint" can be as much of a blessing as the birth of a child.

Even spiritual eyes need to be refocused from time-to-time. A Christ-like mind of a single-minded soldier needs clarity and oneness of thought and our Spirit-led life needs a new and sure reinforcement.

Songs and words will help others do that long after the soldier has served his purpose in his own life.

But no matter the circumstances, we must meet them all with anticipation and expectation—not with fear and doubt. By faith in God, ultimately good can come from even the most difficult situations.

Then, we must take an extra step—fully trusting Him—even if we do not *ever* fully understand. We choose to trust him anyway because we know that He is sovereign and always worthy of it. It is only in this trusting context that we can declare with words of certainty that: *"In this life, we may suffer broken bones, but His Words will never harm us."*

These difficult occurrences, along with the details that go with them, are placed in our custody. They must be preserved as part of our testimony for the benefit of others. On occasion, the challenges may be solely for—our own good, but I believe those instances are the exceptions not the general rule.

In the Bible, God told Abraham that He was going to bless him. But it was not a blessing that was just for Abraham. God went on to say that he would be blessed **so that**…he could be a blessing to others (Genesis 12:2, KJV).

As a child of God, everything that happens to us is a blessing from God. Our "blessings" may be birthed from positive or negative encounters, but they are not ours to keep or hide. Our talents, gifts and blessings are to be shared with others to bring glory to God and good to us. So too, our pain and suffering experiences are not ours to conceal and forget. If these difficulties are viewed correctly against the blessed backdrop of God's perfection, they will be equal in glory to God and good to us. We have thus been blessed, so that we can be a blessing. Speak it, write it or put those words to music—but share it.

Should everyone who is blessed write a song or a book? No, they shouldn't do either, if they are not led to. But no matter how we choose to translate our testimony of blessings, we should use the same measure of dedication, consideration and commitment to share our blessing for God's glory. Make your blessings a testimony of your faith increasing through God's faithfulness to you.

You may be blessed with the ability to sing a song or write music. You may author a book, preach it from a pulpit or simply share it in a personal testimony with someone. But, the value of your "testimony bag" depends greatly on what is in it. What do the words of your testimony say? How deep is the meaning? How well have you prepared it in advance? What value does it possess and what effect will sharing your testimony have?

Words are powerful. As we passionately pursue a fuller and deeper relationship with God as single-minded Christian soldiers, our testimony will speak volumes about God and it could eternally...put a song in someone's heart.

I could have shortened this chapter greatly by using only a few words like: "Our testimony usually comes from experiences, both good and bad."

However, it is my sincere hope that not leaving out important words, meanings and illustrations will enable you to see how and why the proper backdrop must...be preserved.

---

[1] *Wonderful Words of Life*, Phillip Bliss, 1874, published in 475 hymnals to date.

22.
Back Drop or Jaw Drop

Strengthening Strategy:
Understanding the consequences of living life on your own terms.

In the last chapter, we discussed that life events can only be identified correctly if they are viewed against the backdrop of God's perfection and His holy standard. The reality of this perception becomes very clear when we use the backdrop of the consequences of a life that is in enmity with God. The difference in impressions becomes so blatantly obvious when you examine those produced from a godly life projected on God's perfect backdrop of peace, love and obedience compared to those made from a life of destruction, sin and chaos. Looking at the two results should cause a physical jaw drop!

In this day and age, attempting to clearly expose wrong in almost any area of life is labeled as not being "politically correct." If you demand a just penalty be paid for a wrong committed against you, you are really radical! You are either a "racist," "unpatriotic" or somewhere in a list of other ugly terms invented to discredit the truth. We must ask ourselves, would we rather be "politically correct" or spiritually right?

To truly be single-minded Christian soldiers, Jesus requires us to imitate Him, to be spiritually accurate and to call people out on their indiscretions in truth and love. Does the story of the woman at the well ring a bell? If not, I suggest you read it in the Gospel of John, Chapter 8.

The world believes there is a much kinder and more gentile approach to dealing with what they call slight indiscretions or minor infractions. The world tells us that our words should be chosen carefully to urge transgressors to simply rethink their path without damaging their fragile psyche. Under no circumstances, should you ever violate someone's space or discredit their individuality.

We are now seeing this "politically correct" stuff spill over into so-called religious circles. From religious literature to sermons on TV, *more emphasis is placed on not offending people than on explaining how much God is offended **by** people.*

Politicians must choose their words very carefully. One wrong word could end a political career that was headed to the White House. My father use to say, *"Politicians don't lie, they just have an amazing ability of telling the truth, several different ways, to keep from lying."*

Pastors must be very careful in their literal interpretation of the Bible. Many pastors, evangelists and Bible teachers today live under a constant barrage of ridicule, persecution and even physical threats against themselves and their families because of the words they use or the truth they preach.

If we refrain from using words that seem too harsh, distasteful or offensive, we dilute the necessity of a backdrop of sin to reveal guilt. We obscure the need for repentance and God's restoration that only His forgiveness can provide.

Those righteous demands of Deity for total restoration on His terms becomes reduced to a mere shadow of His mandate for holiness. God's Word seems hollow and powerless. This kind of "linguistic malpractice" has eternal consequences. When that time comes, only one word becomes the epitaph on the headstone of self-justification and meaningless rhetoric: "Judgment!"

Some words or phrases in the Bible that seem negative are actually not if they are viewed correctly against the alternative. For instance: realizing we are "lost and without hope" sounds terrible by itself. But realizing where we are helps us get directions to where we need to be—saved with Heaven as our guaranteed destination. Here is an example of what I mean: When you go to a new shopping mall for the first time, you may have no clue where the store is that you are looking for. But if you find a map with a directory of the entire mall, a red "X" that marks a spot where you are, along with an arrow beside it and words that say: "You are here."

It is comforting to know where you are. How else can you determine a route if you don't know where you are in relation to your destination? Can you imagine a map without an "X" to mark where you are in relation to where you want to go? Do you turn right or left? Do you go up or down? How far?

Understanding and seeing our "separation" from God clearly helps us realize the need to be reunited with God.

The word blood sounds gruesome until you fully understand how valuable and necessary it is. The shed blood of our Savior washes away our sin and make us clean.

Hymns have been dropped from the hymnal simply because they contain the word blood. Other words that define the clarion call of the Christian life are skimmed over, including: righteousness, sanctification, justification, repentance and holiness.

Some people have thought that these words are too confusing to explain, too difficult to conform to, and that they take too much time to research. However, any Christian who truly seeks to please the Father will pursue all of them.

The world also says some words are too harsh and divisive. They say these words make people feel guilty and make them seek unrealistic goals. Then, when people fail to reach these high goals, this failure can have lasting effects on their sense of well-being. Duh…that changing—often the convicting, motivating effect—is what the words were intended to create! Hello!

Why is examining all these issues and words—both negative and positive—with the proper backdrop of God's Word so important? The reason is that all these words have precisely defined consequences and/or rewards. Only God's Word can clearly define and explain each meaning. That is why the Bible is so adamant about not altering the

Word of God by so much as one period or comma! All of the words and punctuation marks serve a divine purpose with divine accuracy and clarity.

We must begin to see God's words and illustrations as the tools of the surgeon who cuts—not to injure—but with the ultimate goal of healing and restoring life. God, like the surgeon, invades the body with the right motive. He removes those foreign invaders that seek to steal vitality, kill the body and destroy the soul. He must cut out the enemies of life, health and strength and make the crooked straight. He must fix us and transform us so that we can carry out our mission.

The Great Physician is the one who has given us the divinely chosen "Word," meaning His Son, who unlocks the closed doors of our understanding. He brings light to the shadows of our mind and restores life to the lifeless.

We are sternly warned to stay the course. In addition, the backdrop of the Word of God must be kept totally intact so that sin can easily be recognized against it.

Visualize a picture of a white cat, drinking white milk out of a white bowl on a white sheet of paper. Is it hard to make out the details? Now change the backdrop from a white sheet to a black sheet. The subject of the picture becomes quite clear.

As ugly as sin is, the reality of the consequences need to be perfectly clear. The darker we see sin, the brighter God's Word shines. If we lessen the intensity, the clear message of the Gospel will be reduced to a dim shadow, and people won't hear and believe that there is reason to change. Then, they will truly be…left to wonder.

23.
The Bride in Beige: "I'm not Perfect, But I'm Close."

Strengthening Strategy:
Not compromising in purity so that you accurately represent Christ's character.

Tradition says that a new bride should wear white. Just as a soldier's uniform shows the world that he is part of the military, the bride's gown is a symbol of her commitment to remain pure for her one and only—her husband.

Well, I'm confused (now there's a revelation). How is it that 98% of women wear a white wedding dress, but statistics tell us that at least 45% of women confess to having sex before marriage?

If we really want to be "politically correct" shouldn't it be OK to wear beige and make the statement, *"Hey, I'm not perfect, but I'm close?"* Or, *"Don't label me as impure, just think of me as experienced?"*

The Book of Revelation is filled with references to white garments worn by those who are "worthy," "overcomers" in 3:5, even "rich" and "in places of authority" (Revelation 3:4,5,18 and 4:4, KJV). And there are many other "white" references.

More focus must be given to the command for Christians to remain pure. Christian men and women should be pure before marriage. In addition, Christian men and women should remain pure AFTER their spiritual betrothal (salvation) to God, so that they qualify to wear white again in the future. White "raiment," another term for clothing, is mentioned 23 times in Revelation alone. Clearly God thinks wearing white and the purity associated with it is important! Actually, it is more than important...

White clothing is also a <u>reward</u>: *"He that overcometh, the same shall be* **clothed** *in* **white** *raiment; and I will not blot out his name out of the book of life, but I will confess his name before my Father, and before his angels."* (Revelation 3:5, KJV). Does it sound like white raiment is important?

When my wife and I accepted the blessed challenge of teaching youth and young adult Sunday school classes together, I did not foresee that marriage counseling would be such a major part of the job description.

It seemed that no matter what the Bible study topic was for the week, the conversation always came back to dating and marriage—talk about "hormone city!"

I might be teaching about the significance of the Ashes of the Red Heifer in relation to end-time prophecy, and yep...somehow we would end up talking about marriage, dating and relationships.

People often navigate today's dating culture by categorizing their prospects based on opinions developed during a relatively short period of time. It is usually quick and simple: we observe, listen a little and then label. Bang! That's it. The faster you can do that, the better. You make an instant mental classification and you are on to the next prospect. Boy, that's a rather "beige" way to look at dating.

And, if meeting someone in your sphere of influence isn't fast enough for you, you can go online to several match-making sites and let them do the presorting for you.

(The Bible strongly cautions against match-making in the Book of Leviticus, which says that it is "sorcery." But that is a sermon for another day...I'm just sayin'...)

I will simply state that I believe that relying on the Holy Spirit to help us discern the future of relationships is an absolute necessity. You can't substitute a website and there is no app for Holy Spirit discernment.

Many of us have heard the overly used sales pitch, *"You only have one chance to make a first impression."* Well, acting on your first impression when you are buying a tomato at the market may be OK, but we should not rely on that process for formulating our impressions of people.

Forming first impressions can become a lazy habit and it is difficult to change perceptions that are initially carved in stone. So, be slow to engrave them in your mind prematurely. I have had good first impressions turn out badly and not so good impressions prove me totally wrong over time.

(For example, if you would have relied on your first impression about my book, you probably wouldn't be reading this part!)

Keep this process about the importance of forming impressions about people in mind when the first opportunity to witness to a non-believer occurs. First impressions are really important in talking with non-believers because the opportunity to share our faith does not present itself very often. People that God calls us to witness to need to see "white," not beige. You may not get another chance.

Therefore, we must make sure that our first impression is great. But, just in case it is not, your second, your third and every impression must also be prepared in advance.

Let's take another look at how important it is to be pure in heart through obedience and preparation. The seriousness of this foresight is alluded to in Jesus' parable about the 10 virgins in Matthew's Gospel, the first book of the New Testament. In this story, the virgin brides who had been preparing for their grooms and remaining pure were at home, ready with oil they needed.

They were ready to answer the Bridegroom's invitation and go with Him to the feast when He called at a moment's notice. Those who had oil were assured a place with the Bridegroom—they were secured in His presence for eternity. Those who were not prepared were shut out from the feast (Matthew 25:1–13, KJV).

This story represents how God calls us to be prepared in advance with pure hearts and minds. We must be filled with His Oil (which the Bible often uses as a reference to the Holy Spirit), clean, properly dressed in purity and ready for the Bridegroom, who symbolizes Jesus, to appear.

Another exhortation to be pure is found in the last chapter of the Book of Revelation, the last chapter of the New Testament. The verse states that an Angel came to John and said, *"Come hither, I will shew thee the bride, the Lamb's wife"* (Revelation 21:9, KJV).

John is showing us the Bride of Christ, which is the church, made up of believers who are adorned in white. We are expected to provide the most accurate representation of His character as possible. The only way we can acquire that purity is through the power of the Holy Spirit.

If we were to take a closer look at those people who present a less than beautiful bride-like impression of the church, we may discover a less than ideal situation in their own marriages or lives here on earth as well.

When marriages of people in our churches are in turmoil, their spiritual garments become aged and beige like an old photograph. Their robes, which are supposed to be pure and holy to represent their allegiance to Christ, could appear dingy and coffee stained.

Therefore, providing a strong platform for Christ-centered marriages is an effective resource to help marriages stay biblically grounded. Strong marriages will keep the church strong, pure and ready to wear white for all eternity.

As single-minded Christian soldiers, we are called to be pure in heart, which will keep our "white" uniforms pressed and clean. First impressions will be lasting ones. There will be no question of who we are…in this life or the life thereafter.

24.

Love and Marriage

Strengthening Strategy:
Fitting together like a horse and carriage.
Well...Yes and maybe—or maybe not.

The song actually goes like this..."*Love and marriage, love and marriage...goes together like a horse and carriage...*" Well, yes—and maybe.

"God Love," like the love we discussed in the previous chapter, is the foundation for good marriages. The horse and carriage part? That works best when the horse is in the front! Let's sort this love thing out so that we can be single-minded in marriage, which is an important area of life. Let's start by putting first things first...

I am going to draw on my own experience and practice in life counseling as a pastor. I never perform a marriage ceremony unless the couple agree to a few things first. Even before we talk about the multifaceted and complex topic called "love," there is something else we must discuss: their personal relationships with God.

I want to make sure those waiting to be wed are spiritually compatible. My prayer is that any marriage be built with the correct foundation before they start hanging wall paper and making babies.

As good as my own marriage is, it actually helps me understand just how bad a bad marriage could be if God were not in it.

Next, the marital counseling session also begins with a change in their geographical location. This rule may be sound a bit trivial or extreme, but it is a good idea for the couple to sit apart. No "kissie-face" or "huggie-bear" is allowed during the sessions. Their hormone levels are already out the roof and cuddling is definitely a distraction. It makes it hard for them to focus. (It is fairly distracting for me, too!)

Now that they are in the right positions and the pleasantries are out of the way, I begin with the next question: *"Why do you want to get married?"* They usually look at each other with the puppy dog look and sigh…and one of them says, *"Because we are in love…and we can't live without each other. We want to be with each other for the rest of our lives."* You can almost hear the Hallmark commercial in the background. Unfortunately, I have yet to hear, "Because this person is who God told me I should marry."

Let me share a nugget of wisdom from my own courtship experience and my father-in-law's interaction with us. When Kaye and I decided to tell her parents about our decision to marry, I will never forget what her father said to me. But for you to get the full impact of this monumental act of courage on my part, I must properly set the stage for you…

I have to approach a Baptist minister, who is also my pastor. He stands a good six inches taller than me and outweighs me by about 80 pounds. I am used to hearing him pound the pulpit on occasion as he preaches like the Army of the Lord is coming any minute! On a few occasions, I believe I saw lightning come out of his eyes and his hair was on fire!

So, "yours truly" must find the right time to inform him of my plan to take his daughter from him, and I need to make him excited about the idea.

Being the realist that I am, I have already gone over all the possible answers and results (including prolonged physical impairment). Was I afraid? Not me! I march forward in the strength of my love for my woman. (Love has a way of empowering even the weakest of men.) After all, I had already survived two tours in Vietnam. Hey, I'm the man and I'm going for it! Yes Sir! I feel 10-feet tall, bullet-proof and determined.

What he said to me took me so off guard that it literally left me speechless. He said, *"Well son, it's a pleasure to finally meet you. I have been praying for you for over 18 years."*

I almost fell over! It never occurred to me to pray for my future wife once in a while, let alone every day for the past 18 years—and this man had been praying for me all that time! Our relationship was an answer to his prayer! (Praise God it was not a reason for me to visit the E.R.)

But, let's get back to my experiences in marriage counseling...During the next few sessions, the couple and I cover many important topics—up to and including—old age. Almost without fail, when we are finished, the countenance of the blissful couple has changed to: *"Wow, we never really thought about all that stuff. We just want to be together!"*

I hate to burst the lovebirds' bubble, but God is serious about marriage, and any two planning on entering into it need to take a very close look at what God has to say about the topic. Those of us who are already married could probably benefit from a reminder as well.

God initiated marriage in the book of Genesis. He explained the plan, the purpose and the ultimate goal of the union between a man and woman to Adam and Eve. Here is a very brief outline of it.

God's plan for marriage:
- Is initiated by Him.
- Consists of one male and one female.
- Includes Him choosing which female and which male will go together.
- Is a covenant the couple enters with God.

God's purpose for marriage is:
To make the couple be fruitful and multiply so that they glorify God by representing Him well.

God's ultimate process for marriage is:
To train them to raise up "God-men," a term that means men and women who first have a personal relationship with God and who then

Love and Marriage

equip others with the knowledge and truth of God. Then, they are to give birth to—and raise up—the next generation to repeat the same process.

God's ultimate goal of marriage is:
To receive the glory He deserves from His creation that willfully chooses to worship and praise Him in that covenant.

How did all this go down with the first couple? I am sure there was an attraction between Adam and Eve that God placed within them. But did you notice, He *never* said that He gave Eve to Adam because Adam loved her.

Affection was a by-product of the God-ordained relationship. Remember this principle: love is a command to obey, not a feeling to entice. (We will take a closer look at this statement in the next chapter).

If you reduce love to a mere attraction or feeling, you miss the *source* of real love. God "IS" love and He commands us to duplicate it, in His way.

We cannot allow feelings of affection, lust, physical attraction, money, fame, sudden bursts of insanity, hormone spikes or even a touch of nausea to be mistaken for love. Nor should any of these feelings be the catalyst for marriage and babies! True "God-love" will come when the two people who *He chooses* come together in total obedience to a divine selection. Together, the two will live out His call on their lives.

When the Bible says, *"Seek ye first the Kingdom of God and all these things shall be added unto you..."* (Matthew 6:33, KJV), it includes marriage! If your primary goal is a "Kingdom of God marriage," then *"all these things,"* meaning the blessed by-products of pleasing the Father first, will be added unto you. You will receive things like the deep and lasting affection that most people mistake for the initial warm and fuzziness of human attraction.

Seek God and be open to recognize and welcome a union that was designed by Him before you were born. You must prayerfully, carefully and spiritually seek His choice for a spouse for you. And out

124

of that union, love, companionship, children, a dog, mortgage and credit card debt will mysteriously appear. All of that will happen at the right time, in the right proportion—all for your enjoyment!

In addition, there will be blessed by-products that include unending romance, true love, great sex, financial blessings, perfect companionship, honesty and integrity in relationships, and on, and on and on. All of these fantastic blessings are based on acting upon and *being in* "God-love" with Him *and* with your spouse. This part of the promised reward will help you remain pure—as described in the preceding chapter.

All the blessings of a loving marriage relationship were birthed in the mind of God eons ago. They are NOT the laundry list you make up in advance of getting hitched. If the main reason you get married is fulfill your dream of a pre-conceived fairytale romance, you may be starting on shaky ground!

Making these decisions before we have to face them will keep us from spur-of-the-moment reactions. Rather, we should be prepared to act upon a pre-determined, single-minded decision to obey God that won't…leave anything out.

25.
Loving for a Lifetime

Strengthening Strategy:
Committing to obey instead of relying on feelings.

What will you do when the "warm and fuzzies" in your marriage fade? Because they might. What will you do when the money runs out? Because it could. How will you handle it when your physical appearance and body begins to change? Because they absolutely do. I am reminded of how my body has changed every morning when I bend over to tie my shoes. (Praise God for slip-ons, polyester and Velcro!)

All these questions are ones that I ask couples in my office for premarital counseling, because I have seen how important and overlooked they are.

Two other important but related lessons that I try to get across to couples are a mouthful, but full of Peltier wisdom:

1) *"Happiness is what happens when everything that happens, happens to happen...happily. But, when things happen that are not anything to be happy about, you better have joy. You better have the right mate and you better be committed to obey until the end."*

2) *"Joy is what gets you through when everything that happens to you...happens, unhappily. If you have that joy, (the joy that can only come in a relationship with God), then unhappy circumstances will not affect your marriage, your life or your outlook on the future. In fact, hard times will reinforce or even strengthen your marriage."*

I have had people who have been married for years come into my office and tell me, *"I just don't feel loved anymore,"* or *"I don't feel the love I had for him/her like I used to."* What a perfect time for a Denoso smack in the back of the head (spiritually speaking, of course).

My initial thought is they need to repent of their foolish and immature concept of love, AND LOVE ANYWAY! **Love is not something you feel, it is something you elect to "do" and "be" in obedience to God.**

But, don't take my word for it. Let's look at the Apostle Paul's words in Scripture: *"Husbands, love your wives"* (Ephesians 5:25, KJV). That statement is a **command**, not a feeling. The initial way that we think of as love may or may not be earned, deserved or felt at the time. It doesn't matter. You entered into a covenant relationship, so love in obedience to it.

Quit sinning and **decide** to love as you are commanded to do. Do not confuse love with lust, fondness or anything else. Love is a verb and a noun. It is a decision of obedience and a sentiment to express!

Thinking about God's action may help you obey and love anyway…I know it helps me. I remember that God did not love me because I was handsome, intelligent or funny, even though all those qualities are true to a certain degree. He made the decision in spite of me. Similarly, no justification or feelings warrant God's love for you…because God decided to love you when you were quite…unlovely. In fact, he "foreknew" you and loved you before you were even created. "Foreknew" means he was able to look into the future before you were ever born and decided to love you. He knew what you needed and made provision for your need in advance. How's that for love?

He made all of us in His image, and He calls us to love in the same way that He loves us. What God expects about how we love our spouses is clear.

In Matthew's Gospel, the question is asked *"Teacher, which is the great commandment?"* Then, an answer is given, *"You **shall** love the LORD your*

God with all your heart" (Matthew 22:36–37, NKJV, bold emphasis from this author).

The greatest *command* is that you *shall,* not may or could or even should. It is a divine command that you must obey. **Therefore, love for your spouse is an act of obedience to God.** Attraction, affections and lust are totally different.

Stay with me on this ever-so important topic…Set aside your preconceived ideas about love and romance and open up a little. Be kinda like my grandson when he wants to get his point across. He decides to hug his Nana to get her undivided attention and says with outstretched arms, *"OK Nana, bring it in!"*

Let's also look at the words carefully in John's Gospel: *"This is My **commandment, that you love** one another **as I have loved you"*** (John 15:12, NKJV, bold emphasis from this author). We must love like God loves. It is a decision to "be" like God, to not just to have an attraction you may be inclined to consider based on feelings. Can one word be a verb and a noun at the same time? Yup, you bet your ecclesiastical boots you can. (I do love that word, ecclesiastical!)

Finally, marriage is a holy covenant, and it is a three-way contract between God and the two people who become married. "Marriages are made in Heaven" is a true saying. That is why we call it a marriage covenant.

Being single-minded Christian soldiers and playing our roles as part of the "bride" of Christ wearing white will make a great first impression to others who are watching. If our hearts are pure and our own marriages stay grounded in Christ-centered love, others may actually understand the importance of marriage in this life as well as the significance of being HIS bride for eternity.

Let's do our part to ensure that God is honored and the real concept of love and marriage is not…overshadowed by the Enemy's ploy.

Otherwise, those who are watching won't want to have their own godly marriages. Their path of enjoying the authentic, heavenly love that God designed them for may be…missed entirely.

26.
A Court-Martial Offense

Strengthening Strategy:
Knowing the dangers of micromanaging supernatural inspiration, authority and
leadership...a slippery slope.

You will have to allow me a little latitude for just a moment. I want to focus the next two chapters primarily on pastors, preachers, teachers and evangelists—those who are called to be the leaders of single-minded Christian soldiers. These next two chapters are a bit heavy, but I believe they are necessary.

It is important for those of us who are leaders to remember who we work for and who we are accountable to. Even if you do not fall into one of the categories mentioned above, this chapter will help you as well so don't skip it.

When an offense in the military is bad enough, it becomes a court-martial offense. In the civilian world, a court-martial would be equivalent to a felony at the federal level, or the worse kind of offense. A court-martial often results in serious penalties, which include being stripped of rank and/or dishonorably discharged from military service.

One pastor explained how this idea of how God's originally appointed men and "court martialing" could go together rather well, I thought. He was preaching about how God had very specific instructions about how the Ark of the Covenant (that contained the law of God) was to be physically transported. Because the Ark, which was gold plated and a box like structure, was too holy to be touched, the pastor said, "It was to be *carried* on poles *by men.*" What he meant was that God's presence (in the Ark itself) was never intended to be moved or touched by "boards" and *"big wheels!"* Now, that's funny! Well, not really, because that Old Testament story ended with the offender touching it and committing the highest offense—just like a court martial—he was struck down and killed by God. (You can read more about that incident in the next chapter.)

The reason for the story is to show that God's original order was given to the man that He had selected to lead the people. His man was responsible directly to God to see that the message was delivered and the order was obeyed. If he did not carry out his orders, the God-appointed man was subject to court-martial by his Commanding Officer: God and God alone. This was the way spiritual leadership is supposed to work. We should be more concerned about answering to God, than we are about answering to man or men on a "board."

Today in churches, however, pastors can face their demise from the judgment of people on "boards." They can be cautioned, restrained and even fired by "boards." We have boards for this and a board of directors for that. Many organizations have boards and a lot of "big wheels" running them.

So, how did "boards" come about?

Moses started the whole delegation of authority thing when he was trying to lead God's people out of bondage. I think it may have been one of those days when he was hot, tired from walking and had a lot of sand in his sandals. The combination of a little heat exhaustion and all the whining and excuses must have frustrated the holiness right out of him. So, he threw up his hands in disgust and sought another way to deal with the problem.

He may have thought, *"I'm so bored with all this trivial junk, I think I'll give the people a 'board' of their own to handle this stuff."* Bingo, the Official "Board of Directors—Desert Division for Whining and Complaining" was established. Later, the board was expanded to include the sub-division of "needies" and the "greedies" and so on.

God did not assemble a board of directors on the mountain to discuss the Ten Commandments either. Nor did He lay out a marketing plan and take a vote to elect Moses as leader of this epic 40-year National Geographic Adventure. He personally called Moses to do it—all of it.

Yes, God did agree to give Aaron to Moses as a helper in the human resources department as a communications specialist, but even that was birthed out of Moses' whining. (Apparently, Moses thought his speech impediment "thingie" was something God may have missed during the initial interview.)

Our human tendency is to micromanage everything! God gave us the Ten Commandments and after that, we started helping God out with another list of rules and then we added a few hundred additional regulations. (That listmania sounds like the IRS tax code!) The trouble is, not one human in a billion years could ever come close to successfully complying with the first Ten Commandments!

In addition, we have "religious auditors," who keep records and the "congregational union bosses" to control us. We would be much better off if we would just quit helping God so much. If there was ever a bumper sticker sent from Heaven, it would read…*'Please! Stop helping me!"*

Moses could have made the job easier if he would have said, *"Hey! All you knuckleheads listen up. God said to knock off the foolishness or we're going to be out here in the desert for quite a while and the menu is going to be really limited."*

Like Moses, pastors garner very little respect. In fact, they don't get invited *to* lunch, they *are* lunch! Wouldn't it be great if the pulpit was manned by some real Spurgeon power again? How about if we experienced some of D.L. Moody's passion or some of Billy Sunday's boldness? Do you think that we could get away with that today?

This lack of respect that leaders face is partially because we don't really expect it, teach it or demand it. Unfortunately, some pastors don't deserve it because they have become more concerned about answering to a "board" than answering a heavenly call!

Well, excuse me! Pastors are heavenly-ordained ambassadors of the Most High God, and the last thing we should be worried about is what any person or any "board" can do to us. And yet, many pastors are more concerned with the possibility of being sacked than they are about grieving the Holy Spirit through compromise and fear. They are more willing to go with mob rule than to stand alone with Christ on a hill.

I'm not saying that we pastors should not take counsel from the wise. In fact, I think it shows great wisdom on behalf of the pastor if he does seek **wise** counsel and surrounds himself with the godly influence of dedicated, seasoned and spirit-filled Christ followers.

Let's put this issue in the proper prospective. Ministers have accepted divine calls on their human lives. They carry out supernatural appointments to natural men for a supernatural challenge. The challenge is to minister to a flock of diverse followers who come from all walks of life and have their own opinions. (It has to be a call from Heaven, because no one in their right mind would even entertain that thought here on Earth!) Herding cats with a steam-roller would be easier.

The Creator of the Universe has called pastors to a job that is a Holy Spirit-empowered position of responsibility and authority. This job requires them to speak on behalf of the God of Heaven to earthly inhabitants with absolute accuracy and authority. He also commands that His message be presented with boldness, and that it be proclaimed without hesitation or apology.

I was a bi-vocational pastor for almost six years. For those of you who do not know what "bi-vocational" means, it is serving a church full-time as pastor, for part-time pay, while working two full-time jobs somewhere else so that you can eat.

It is very hard work, but as a bi-vocational pastor, with your full-time pay not tied to your words, you can "afford" to be bold—no pun intended.

By-the-way, just so you know, there is no such a thing as part-time church work. I pastored my church like a full-timer, while owning and operating two businesses that I started from scratch. I'm not complaining about the part-time pay, I'm just explaining the reality of the situation to make a point.

I must be honest and admit that I rather enjoyed the freedom of knowing that I did not have to depend on my small love gift from the church for survival. While that statement may sound petty, I enjoyed a freedom that many pastors will never experience. I used to tell people, *"I make my living selling **insurance** but my passion is giving **assurance** away for free!"*

Having another way to support myself enabled me to truly feel free to stick to what God was telling me to preach. I never worried about losing my job as a pastor or missing a paycheck. I preached what I felt was right. I preached it the way that I felt it needed to be preached and I got in people's faces when I thought they needed it. (Of course, it was always under the strict leadership and direction of the Holy Spirit, and I always operated out of a heart of compassion, tempered with love and joy…Praise God and Amen!)

I cannot imagine trying to pastor a church in fear of the meeting that was coming on Monday morning. I can't imagine sitting there, listening to a sermon analysis and debates over my management decisions of the past few week as I attempt to answer interrogating questions from a "board!"

As pastors have less and less authority, they become more and more likely to lose their jobs. If people are allowed to continue micromanaging supernatural inspiration, authority and leadership completely out of the equation, a pastor/shepherd will be reduced to a "vocational choice" of employment and not a "divine call" on the lives of men.

Diminishing the high calling of a pastor will hinder the movement of the Spirit of God in any congregation. Where there is no freedom for the Spirit of God to control the emotions, teach the mind and direct the will, anarchy will result and churches will die.

Some organized churches may still exist as a monument to their own creative abilities. Some churches even flourish and experience measured success by man's yardstick. But there will be very little heavenly value in their accomplishments.

God will examine them and deliver a verdict: *"For you say, I am rich; I have prospered and grown wealthy, and I am in need of nothing; and you do not realize and understand that you are wretched, pitiable, poor, blind, and naked"* (Revelation 3:17, AMPC).

We need to re-establish a healthy respect for God's divinely chosen representative. It is not just a courtesy: It is required in the Word of God.

"Let the elders that rule well be counted worthy of double honour, especially they who labour in the word and doctrine" (1 Timothy 5:17, KJV).

We must apply this verse by holding our pastors in this highest esteem, and not let this recognition be…left out.

27.

Hot Dog Accountability

Strengthening Strategy:
Being accountable to "a higher authority."

This chapter ties in with the previous chapter, but hang in there, it is different…

Churches hold the pastor accountable—and that is a good thing—to an extent. All single-minded Christian soldiers need some measure of accountability, and a pastor is no exception. This situation is like the ad for **_Hebrew National Hot Dogs,_** where the company claims that not all hot dogs are equal. Since the meat from this Hebrew organization is kosher, they are held to a higher standard. The pastor is also "accountable to a higher standard." Yes, there are—and should be—checks and balances. The standard, however, is the Word of God, not individual opinions, collective majorities or wealthy minorities.

What is not good is when God's children make decisions that are not Spirit-led. Instead, they conger up self-serving agendas based on personal preference rather than biblical mandates.

This discussion reminds me of a comment that I heard an old "Hell, fire and brimstone" preacher make about 40 years ago. I thought it was funny then, but it has since become etched in my mind and I have applied it regularly.

It was during a Wednesday night business meeting, when the discussion about whether to keep a particular program going or to drop it, developed into a full-blown argument.

The pastor had kept quiet and let the people vent for about 15 minutes when he could not take it any longer. He rose to his feet and said, *"It does not matter in what state a dead body lies. Resurrect it or bury it, but get on with what matters!"* The church dropped the lifeless program and focused its efforts in a new direction.

Here is a word of caution: When you place yourself in a position to personally hold God's man accountable and impose your perceptions, directions and visions on him, you are playing with supernatural matches, and you will get burned.

If you reach out to steady the ark, you may get a stiff punishment like Uzzah got back in the Old Testament after he disobeyed God's <u>specific instructions NOT to touch the ark</u>.

*"And when they came to Nachon's threshing floor, Uzzah put forth his hand to the **ark** of God, and took hold of it; for the oxen shook it. And the anger of the Lord was kindled against Uzzah; and God smote him there for his error; and there he died by the **ark** of God"* (2 Samuel: 4–5, KJV).

If you reach out to grab heavenly things with human hands, the results can be deadly. It doesn't even matter what your motive may be, you too are still held to a higher standard.

Does this concept of death for disobedience seem harsh to you? Well, maybe it is, in human thinking. But God is not interested in human opinion; He is interested in absolute obedience and you better not touch things He regards as holy.

God calls leaders according to His divine plan and purpose for their lives. Scripture is very explicit and detailed concerning holy calls. Likewise, you better not touch them either!

Therefore, I encourage you to research the verses in the Bible referring to God's calling of priests and leaders of the church. I might also mention, if you don't see your name listed there as the official "Holy Spirit Representative," you may want to back up a bit and take a seat. You will be much safer there.

A **grave** danger lurks when a person who isn't called leads. It is equally as catastrophic when people who aren't called to lead drive out someone who is. And, just in case you were wondering, I did not use the word "grave" by accident. I do believe many people are physically dead and many churches are spiritually dead prematurely because they did not grasp the seriousness of these holy issues.

I witnessed this personally in a church that I was a member of. This church was leading the entire State, in almost every category. They were moving, doing, baptizing and growing to more than 600 weekly attenders.

A few men began to complain about how long the pastor preached. Then they wanted to tell him what he should preach, and it got ugly. They mistreated the pastor, falsely accused him of some things and made some demands that were contrary to his belief. The bottom line was...they ran him off.

At this writing, it has been more than 40 years since that pastor left. That church has never regained even a slight foothold. It has continually declined and it currently has about 15 in attendance on a good day. The church is as dead as a hammer and it cannot even afford to fix the pot holes in the parking lot!

Although church boards tend to overarch their authority and oust pastors too easily, they church governing bodies place little to no "accountability" upon church members. Perhaps we should take one page out of the Catholic Church's playbook and apply it to this problem. The Catholic Church will "excommunicate" people because of offenses like creating a schism or divide, like what I witnessed in my former church.

For those of you who don't know what "excommunication" means, it doesn't mean they just quit inviting them to the Tupperware parties and remove their names from the Christmas card list. Excommunication is a much more serious process. It means the person gets cut off, thrown out of the church and sent to purgatory or the Walmart's Customer Service Counter...depending on how serious the offense was.

Many pastors know and can prove that some church members are engaged in activities that are absolutely against the Word of God. Unfortunately, many church governing bodies today cannot and/or will not hold members accountable even if the pastor has made the offense known. Then, we wonder why there is only a shadow of godliness without any power being displayed through our congregations.

The matter is plain and simple: **Not** holding individuals and/or churches accountable is contrary to Scripture. We can see this truth by looking at a well-known biblical example of a godly leader who holds a sinner accountable.

Joshua had replaced Moses as the leader of God's people. Unlike Moses, Joshua was a mighty warrior. He was winning every battle, every skirmish—and seemed unbeatable—no matter the odds.

All of a sudden, he was defeated. Joshua realized the Lord's presence was no longer with him and his troops. God revealed to Joshua what the problem was—someone in the camp had sinned. It wasn't Joshua or anyone in the army that he had led into battle, it was someone back at the campsite that had disobeyed God. Hidden sin had caused Joshua's entire army to be defeated.

Joshua stopped the war and went back to camp. He searched until he found the offender; HE HELD HIM ACCOUNTABLE and then went back to the battlefield. You can read more in Joshua, Chapter 7 about how Joshua held Achan accountable—and how he used it as a lesson for the whole camp—for this costly sin. But here's the bottom line:

Where there is unchallenged sin in the camp, victors become defeated. A battle or skirmish could be lost today, just like it was for Joshua.

What are a couple key points that church leaders can take away about the importance of accountability?

First, pastors cannot preach messages that are more "seeker sensitive" than "sinner shaking." God does not wink at this watering down of His Word from the pulpit, and second, pastors have to execute all of God's standards and keep people accountable.

Leaders, please, hear me! God has called you as a shepherd! Stop fearing sheep that cannot bite! Be fearful instead, of the lion that goes around seeking to devour you by intimidating you. The Enemy will pressure you to share a more palatable Gospel, delivered from a position of fear. But, stand strong and fight using the superior power given to you by the Lion of Judah! He has won your battle! Stop being defeated and assume the position of His victory!

And to sheep, I say…be sheep. Be great sheep! (If there were no sheep, there would be no need for shepherds.) Remember: sheep eat grass, not one another.

Pastors, pray for the courage of Christ when you learn about the sin that people commit and must be dealt with because the sin of omitting accountability is just as bad. Dealing with these matters is our responsibility and God will judge us for it!

As Paul says, *"For this reason I am writing these things while absent from you, so that when I come, I will not need to deal severely [with you], in my use of the authority which the Lord has given me [to be used] for building you up and not for tearing you down"* (2 Corinthians 13:10, AMPC).

As shepherds, we are directly accountable to "go" in response to His divine appointment. However we must make it perfectly clear that every soldier is in the battle and must also be accountable, even if they are on the front line, like a pastor is.

New recruits are accountable to seasoned veterans—seasoned veterans to their pastor shepherds—and shepherds to the Great Shepherd, our God. There is a chain of command to be followed and not a link in the chain can be…left behind.

28.
Being a Member at the YMCA Is Not Enough

Strengthening Strategy:
Committing to a church.

When you join something, you show your support by committing to it. When you enlist in your country's armed forces, you have to take an oath to serve. Single-minded Christian soldiers also have to take an oath and demonstrate such a commitment.

God commands that His soldiers carry out two of His central purposes with their lives. These two purposes are only done effectively with the support of a good, Bible believing church. Here are God's commands to us:

1) **The Greatest Commandment**: *Jesus said… "'You shall **love the LORD** your God with all your heart, with all your soul, and with all your mind.' This is the first and great commandment. And the second is like it: 'You shall **love your neighbor** as yourself.' On these two commandments hang all the Law and the Prophets." (Matthew 22:36–40, NKJV, bold emphasis from this author).*

2) **The Great Commission**: ***Go and make disciples** of all nations, **baptizing them** in the name of the Father and of the Son and of the Holy Spirit, and **teaching them** to obey everything I have commanded you. And surely I am with you always, to the very end of the age."* (Matthew 28:19–20, NIV, bold emphasis added from this author).

Now, as we start to digest these Scriptures, let's be honest, we may have experienced trying to live the Christian life by ourselves and found that it can very difficult. That difficulty might be because God never intended us to do it alone. In fact, many times He tells us to seek out the wise counsel of others and to be in fellowship with one another. But, that's another topic for another writing.

For now, let's look at the preceding two colossal Scriptures a little closer. We will see how they tell us to involve God and others as part of our Christian walk:

- To "love God with all your heart" is WORSHIP.
- To "love your neighbor as yourself" is SERVICE.
- To "go and make disciples" is EVANGELISM.
- To "baptize" is to INCORPORATE.
- To "teach them to obey everything" is DISCIPLESHIP.

Now, take a minute and list all the people you know—outside of the church—who are:

- Self-motivated worshipers of God on a regular basis...by themselves.
- Actively involved in serving their neighbors...by themselves.
- Making disciples by teaching the Scriptures...by themselves.
- Baptizing people...on their own.
- Doing whatever it takes to get these people involved in a church family...on their own.
- Discipling others as much as it takes, as long as it takes...on their own.

Your list should be about the size of a postage stamp. It doesn't make sense to think anyone could—or would—have that kind of self-motivation and/or resources.

The church is described in the Bible as an organism that is living, breathing and fully functional. It is not a lifeless cinderblock square. It is not a place where people, who don't have anything else to do, visit once in a while to sing and eat.

The church, as Christ ordained it, is multifaceted, but with a clear purpose: to testify of the things of God and to do His will. The church is much like your own body. Lots of parts are working together for a common goal—to move you forward without falling on your face.

The following bulleted text is an actual church statement (which is also known as a church covenant). The name is different, but the concept is the same. It is a statement or agreement documenting what a particular community believes and are committed to do. This particular example starts with worship:

- We believe worship should be spiritual—we are sensitive to the leadership of the Holy Spirit.
- We believe worship should be inspirational— so we give great place to music.
- We believe worship should be intelligent—so we place a great emphasis on teaching the Word of God.
- We believe worship should be fruitful—so we strive to be a manifestation of what we believe and look for results in our own lives that produce God-fruit.

This community went on to describe how they worship through celebration, inspiration, preparation, expression, singing, shouting, clapping, hand raising, kneeling and giving. Try to do all that by yourself! If you can, all you need is a donation cup and a funny hat. You can stand on the street corner and entertain for tips.

Paul, the Apostle tells us: *"There is one body and one Spirit…one Lord, one faith, one baptism; one God and Father of all"* (Ephesians 4:4–6, NKJV).

I believe we need to become part of that *oneness*, which is only found in the one, true church body.

We are to join what is already there. We do not join to lend all of our talents, gifts and ideas to help remake a church into something we prefer.

We are commanded to commit to support our church body with all of our resources. We are to help build that body by actively engaging in its work for Christ. His church is His family. Paul also tells us: *"You are members of God's very own family, citizens of God's country, and you belong in God's household with every other Christian"* (Ephesians 2:19, TLB). It doesn't get any plainer than that!

I have had people tell me that they don't go to church because, *"It is full of hypocrites."* Well, then there's always room for one more! Your own physical body isn't perfect either, but you need as many parts as possible to function. Try leaving a leg at home tomorrow when you go to work, and see how that works for you.

The following list is a collection of benefits that you simply cannot get without belonging to a local body. Every Christians needs:

- A sense of belonging: "So then, as occasion and opportunity opens up to us, let us do good [morally] to all people [not only being useful or profitable to them, but also doing what is for their spiritual good and advantage]. Be mindful to be a blessing, especially to those of the household of faith [those who belong to God's family with you, the believers]" (Galatians 6:10, AMPC).

- Encouragement: "And let us consider and give attentive, continuous care to watching over one another, studying how we may stir up (stimulate and incite) to love and helpful deeds and noble activities" (Hebrews 10:24, AMPC).

- Accountability: "Iron sharpens iron; so a man sharpens the countenance of his friend [to show rage or worthy purpose]" (Proverbs 27:17, AMPC). Accountability to one another sharpens both parties and keeps them on their toes.

- God's presence: "For wherever two or three are gathered (drawn together as My followers) in (into) My name, there I Am in the midst of them" (Matthew 18: 20, AMPC).

- Power: "Again I tell you, if two of you on earth agree (harmonize together, make a symphony together) about whatever [anything and [everything] they may ask, it will come to pass and be done for them by My Father in heaven" (Matthew 18:19, AMPC).

- Unity: "That they all may be one, [just] as You, Father, are in Me and I in You, that they also may be one in Us, so that the world may believe and be convinced that You have sent Me" (John 17:21, AMPC).

- Usefulness: "As each of you has received a gift (a particular spiritual talent, a gracious divine endowment), employ it for one another as [befits] good trustees of God's many-sided grace [faithful stewards of the extremely diverse powers and gifts granted to Christians by unmerited favor]" (1 Peter 4:10, AMPC).

- Strength: "In conclusion, be strong in the Lord [be empowered through your union with Him]; draw your strength from Him [that strength which His boundless might provides]." (Ephesians 6:10, AMPC).

- Love: "Husbands, love your wives, as Christ loved the church and gave Himself up for her" (Ephesians 5:25, AMPC).

You could find other verses about the importance of belonging to the church, but you get the idea.

Many man-made organizations do good deeds, and many people commit to them instead of joining a church. However, my Bible tells me that ANYTHING that takes priority over God and His body, is idolatry. Any person, job, or organization…period.

If you *"…love the Lord your God with all your heart and with all your soul and with all your mind (intellect)"* (Matthew 22:37, AMPC), there shouldn't be any room for anything or anyone else. Everything will be derived from an outpouring of loving God. This statement also reminds us that nothing else can ever take first place over God.

Not to adhere to the requirements of membership is to dilute the concept of the family (the body), which was established by God in the Garden of Eden. Refusing to become a church member is disobedient to a Christ-specific command. Not becoming a member of the local church is really an admission that you are not willing to submit to Christ's ordained body and His commands.

You may be an affiliated *shadow* of the church family, but refusing to obey the command to be a responsible, active, committed and submissive member of the church, results in many prospective church members being...turned off, short-changed and confused. If you are not seriously committed to your faith, why should they seriously consider it?

As a single-minded soldier, let's follow our orders COMPLETELY...let's obey so that we do not make the other parts of the body less effective. Because the less effective the body is, the more chance there is that potential comrades...may be left out.

29.
The Complexity of Simplicity

Strengthening Strategy:
Comprehending the accuracy and divine inspiration of the Bible.

Ok ladies, it's time for a little humor about men because all single-minded soldiers need to be able to laugh at themselves—it's a mandatory life skill. *(I still have to announce my humor to some of you in advance, so get ready, here it comes…)*

Women are amazed that men never read the instructions when they put something together. I have discovered and am convinced that the mental midgets who wrote all instructions are actually communist undercover operatives bent on making everything difficult.

It is all part of the greater plot to overthrow the US via a complex mixture of stressful tactics and frustration that will eventually induce suicidal thoughts. Men believe dynamic and intellectual elite minds of true leaders are being tricked into reading and—attempting to follow—the written instructions that they have been given. Then the rest of mankind will follow.

I picture the whole scenario playing out something like this. . . It's quitting time at the plant in Northern Yuckistan. The production of the first million "Wahootsit's" are complete and ready for shipment. *"It's Friday! Let's get this shipment packaged and out the door!"* the foreman shouts.

Stosh, who is sweeping up a little early, hoping he can get home and milk the goat before dark, asks a simple question in passing that stops the entire crew dead in their tracks: *"You gonna include da instructions with dis?"*

"Oh no!" the foreman responds. *"We forgot the instructions and the guy who usually writes them is doing three to five in Siberia for forging passports. What can we do?"* Guess who they select to write the instructions? *"Yup, congratulations...Stosh, you're the winner!"*

The only requirement for comrade Stosh is to make what should be simple, seem complex and confusing. After he writes up some difficult nonsense, he translates the instructions into Pig-Latin and prints them on recycled tissue paper. He throws in a few extra nuts and bolts that people don't need and leaves out one critical corner piece they do need. The finishing touch includes a metric wrench that resembles a hammer glued to a salad fork!

(Sorry, I got a bit carried away, but these guys make my eyes bleed.)

So let's get back to effective single-minded Christian soldier training, shall we?

So far in this book, we have accumulated quite a list of things that have been "left behind," "left out" or are currently "out of focus." But one of the main reasons these things happen and are left out is because of many Christians' failure to read and study the instruction manual, God's Holy Word. Unlike Stosh's instructions, God's instructions are perfectly complete, creating peace and joy instead of frustration and disillusionment.

Let's look at what one expert has to say about God's Word. Chuck Missler, founder of Koinonia House Ministry based in Coeur d'Alene, Idaho, is an author, evangelical Christian, Bible Teacher, engineer and former business man. He frequently makes the statement, *"The Bible is 66 Books, penned by 40 different authors over 2,000 years without one mistake."* Dr. Missler has numerous messages, videos and teaching DVDs to support his claim.

It is common knowledge that people have spent their entire lives trying to discredit the Bible, but no one has ever been able to find one single error. Think about that. God's Holy Word of instructions does not have one single glitch. The Bible, our instruction manual, has no mistakes, no parts left out and is easy to understand.

(Did you know that the day before the phone book is printed, it is already out of date and the latest and greatest software program has "fixes" coming out the day after it is released?)

The Bible contains the perfect words of The Creator of the Universe: *"Looking unto Jesus the **author** and finisher of our faith"* (Hebrews 12:2, KJV, bold emphasis from this author). These words are perfect and freely given by an all-knowing, Omni-present, uniquely self-sufficient, GOD…to you.

Yes, the Scriptures were penned by human hands—but make no mistake about it—God's hand held those hands as they wrote it. The Bible is a holy, Spirit-empowered, divine manuscript.

With this in mind, do you think God's Word is worth reading? Do you think His instructions are worth following? You bet your ecclesiastical life they are. (Ah, what a multi-functional word, "ecclesiastical"… I love it.)

I have a question for you: Why would anyone attempt to live a Christian life without reading and referring to perfect instructions? God is not just the Author of the perfect instruction manual, but He is also the Creator of the product that the instruction manual was written for: you and me! When you take a minute to think about that, it would be absolutely ridiculous not to read and follow the instruction manual!

Here is a glorious additional bonus to motivate you to read the instructions: In the event you don't completely understand the instructions, you get a free interpreter—the Holy Spirit—provided by God as a bonus!

I love the part of a television infomercial when they say, *"But if you call now, we will double your order."* Well, God is saying, I have not only given you perfect instructions, but since you are calling right now, I'll throw in the perfect interpreter, at no additional cost! What a deal!

Failing to read these perfect instructions makes as much sense as giving your three-year-old a race car. Your child doesn't have adequate training, maturity or experience. And yet, we subject our spiritual lives to the same kind of peril when we don't read the Bible.

We have all heard that the definition of insanity as "doing the same thing over and over and expecting a different result." Well, the definition of insanity applies to the Christian life as well. You cannot ignore the instructions and expect to be a successful follower of Christ. Doing so would be religious insanity. Why has the simplicity of this concept become so complex?

Our Lord gives us a clue to why people make mistakes in this verse: *"Jesus answered and said unto them, Ye do err, not knowing the scriptures, nor the power of God"* (Matthew 22:29, KJV).

In addition to individual Christian insanity, "church insanity" is also rampant. Churches have a tendency to conduct ministry in the same way over and over again, perhaps because it is comfortable, without paying attention to what God requires. And yet, they expect success and God's blessing on the efforts.

Someone gave a pretty good illustration of how far-fetched this idea of anticipating the Lord's blessing is when either an individual or a church operated without His instructions. This person said, *"It is like watching a tornado hit a junk yard and fully expecting to see a completed Boeing 747 aircraft as a result of the storm."*

The Bible is not something to just carry around or place on the end table next to the couch. It should be what **carries you** through every walk of life. God's Word is not a book that eliminates all your problems. But, it does give you answers for your problems, as well as and comfort and strategies for dealing with them. Those who seek the truth are also given favor, as it says in the following verse:

"These were more noble than those in Thessalonica, in that they received the word with all readiness of mind, and searched the scriptures daily, whether those things were so" (Acts 17:11, KJV).

It also makes it easier when you pull your weight with God and not against Him. There are nearly 100 such life instructions in the New Testament alone. One of my favorites is:

"I have told you these things, so that in Me you may have [perfect] **peace** *and confidence. In the world you have tribulation and trials and distress and*

frustration; but be of good cheer [take courage; be confident, certain, undaunted]! *For I have overcome the world. [I have deprived it of power to harm you and have conquered it for you.]"* (John 16:33, AMPC, **bold emphasis from this author**).

This heavenly inspired manual is not just an answer to *your* specific problems. God's Word is the answer to every problem, for every person, in every circumstance, at every time and for all time! Jesus Christ is the cornerstone of our faith that we need to build on. He IS the Word.

May God forgive those of us who would neglect spending time with Him in His Word every day. Let us renew our commitment as single-minded Christian soldiers to personally meet with God right there between the pages of His Word, where He is anxiously waiting for us to spend time with him.

My wife sings a song that really brought this idea home to me. It is titled: "I Miss My Time with You." The song talks about those special times that God spends with us. It describes those intimate moments we share loving on each other. He misses that undivided attention from us. He misses that special time.

I also believe that God misses you during the rough times as well. He misses you when your world crashes in, if you don't come to Him in His Word and meet Him there. The Lord misses an opportunity to see you through the trial, and He misses encouraging you to trust Him through the darkest circumstances. The heavenly Father misses the chance to hang on to you through the storm, when you need healing, restoration and peace.

I believe God also misses His time with His church family. If we neglect the consistent reading and teaching of His Word together in church, we are left to forge ahead in our own human efforts, which are destined to fail. We can become exhausted, frustrated and quit and become totally useless to the Kingdom of God.

The Bible is complex, yet simple enough for everyone to understand if they work at it. The Bible is deep, but will never allow you to sink. It is a sustaining, fulfilling safe harbor in a storm. It is a source of encouragement as well as a love story. The Word of God has poetry and judgment, songs and commandments. It is overflowing with promises and assurance.

So...obey God, who is your Commanding Officer (please also listen to your wife), and read the instruction manual first! Doing so will ensure that whatever project you are working on or whatever life-crisis you are facing will be resolved for His glory and your good...with no pieces left behind.

30.
The Misconception of Conception: Part 1

Strengthening Strategy:
Putting a comma after forgiveness, not a period!

Any editor will tell you that an author should not have to explain his writing to people who have read it. If text has to be clarified after it is read, it could be a sign that the writing style is confusing. So, instead of risking an over-explanation, I'm going to take a different tactic. I'm going to start with telling you what this chapter is **not** about:

It does not discuss the over-politicized, politically correct, legal questions about abortion and women's rights, etc. I believe the Bible is clear on those topics.

What I want to address is the *underlying problem to all of these issues.* As single-minded soldiers, we have to understand what is behind the problem so that we can understand exactly why that problem even exists. This understanding helps us determine how to best proceed as we attempt to fix that problem.

The underlying problem is a large misconception of what "conception" is all about. The bigger picture of conception involves so much more than our perspective about family, children, individual rights and of course, tax deductions.

Misconception for the unsaved person may be the result of parental teaching, educational indoctrination or a simple, selfish desire. For the Christian, misconception may be the result of a deficit in spiritual training and/or a lack of serious study of the Scriptures. But the foundational premise for reproducing as designed by the Creator is not open to human interpretation, understanding or judgment.

Before we move on to unravel this misconception of conception, we have to pause and make something else clear.

I realize that some of you or those close to you may have already had an abortion. So, first let me say with all the love and compassion I can: forgiveness is available for you and this chapter is not intended to condemn you. This chapter is intended to help you move forward with a better understanding from God's prospective.

I do, however, want to also unravel the misconception that anyone who has had an abortion or contributed to one in some way should not be confronted. No one can simply say to another, *"Now it's over, and let's forget it."* Or, *"We should just continue from here, put it behind us, and never speak of it again?"* Absolutely not—on both accounts!

Well then, should you carry the guilt forever as a reminder of it? Should a forgiven soul stay in a position of continual condemnation and dwell in a state of depression? Of course not.

Past sins should instead be viewed through the lens of total forgiveness, made possible because of who Jesus is and His all-saving power. Let's look at this truth in the following verse:

*"Who being the brightness of his glory, and the express image of his person, and upholding all things by the word of his power, when he had by himself **purged** our sins, sat down on the right hand of the Majesty on high."* (Hebrews 1:3, KJV).

Purged means absolved or dismissed…gone! So let's not pick up the guilt that He has died to absolve, OK? What is the point of forgiveness if it is not to restore? What is the point of restoration if it is not to put a person's relationship back to where they were before the transgression? What purpose can an event like this serve? Please think with me about these matters and move away from any pre-conceived ideas you may have.

The Evil One wants to silence you and to destroy the testimony that you now have. He uses guilt and depression to keep you in chains. Some may believe that God has forgiven them but they can't seem to forgive themselves. This feeling is because Satan allows people to look back as much as they want to reinforce guilt. God wants all of His children—including you—to look forward past your forgiveness to the full blessing of restoration.

Nor should the daily struggles of life begin from a position of guilt or fear. It doesn't matter what the sin is—all of them should be considered through the lens of forgiveness and restoration, which is only truly possible through a victorious relationship with Jesus Christ. In fact, **we should put a comma after forgiveness, not a period!**

"Forgiveness" is actually a starting point, not the end of a process. Out with the old and in with the new! The Bible is a book about salvation and **ongoing** restoration. It is all about the forgiveness of sin and the beginning of a new life as a brand new starting point.

If we are to learn from our mistakes and receive forgiveness, *we must also understand what must follow.*

Restoration, however, involves more than just our forgiveness, turning away, never doing the same thing again and feeling better. If that is all our redemption is about, then it is limited to an inward, selfish act. Let's place a comma at forgiveness, instead of a period and follow up our turning away with a positive, outward display of that change.

We must reveal the whole truth about receiving forgiveness and encourage others to do the same. When we become informed where we were previously uninformed, we can press toward sharing the truth and informing others. Let's live our lives and testify about the amazing forgiveness that we receive on an ongoing basis. Our forgiveness, then, becomes an *opportunity and an obligation* to share with others.

Now that we have a more complete picture of forgiveness and restoration that applies to abortion—and every other sin—let's go back to the beginning topic in this chapter.

If we are to have a clear and correct grasp of creation and conception, we must also go back to the beginning to reprogram our basic understanding.

Back to the Book of Genesis, where the purpose for creating man is described as:

- Having communion with Him.
- Living out the marriage covenant.
- Dealing with sin and redemption.
- Blessing man and woman with the command to be fruitful and multiply.

Although the four points above make up a very limited description of creation, they do highlight what is most important for this discussion. The purpose and function of "man" is to raise up redeemed men that will honor, praise and worship a deserving Creator through a God-glorifying personal testimony.

The act of abortion is more than just ending a single life; it is a willful act that demonstrates the exact opposite of God's Will for His creation. It prevents each of the four steps mentioned above from happening.

It is a great achievement in a person's life to acknowledge his fallen state, and to repent and ask for forgiveness. However, there are thousands of people who put a **period** right there, at forgiveness, and never fulfill the remainder of God's plan and purpose for their lives from that point on.

If those people would change the period after forgiveness to a comma, they could continue to live a life that demonstrates not only forgiveness, but also continually testifies of their restoration. By doing "good works" they would enhance their faith, strengthen their walk and build their testimony.

Let us put a comma here too, and say, I will demonstrate my love, my affection, my gratitude and my devotion by living my life as my highest act of worship. I will use my whole life, the good parts **and the bad parts**, to testify of God's plan and purpose for me. MORE COMMAS!

I encourage you to _take advantage of your forgiven sin_ and not allow the Evil One to cut short the redemptive purpose of it. How do we "take advantage of our forgiven sin?" We turn a negative experience into a positive one, which is only possible because God does that within us.

No one encourages someone who has failed more than someone who has and shares a testimony of being forgiven and restored from the same failure. No one can comfort someone who grieves like someone who has been through the grief. Let God use your life-experiences by allowing him to heal you, to move you past these experiences and to move forward…And, as you are on that journey, help others with similar challenges begin to embrace their own healing that is available in Christ.

One of my friends, Kayla Fioravanti, was inspired to help others deal with grief as she processed her own grief. She collected stories, poems and songs that tell transparent stories of authors dealing with grief with open hearts and published *360 Degrees of Grief, Reflections of Hope*, a Selah Press Anthology. The 64 contributing authors, who include Steve Green, Clay and Renee Crosse, Wayne Watson, Kayla Fioravanti and many more, have lived through the complete spectrum of life—from the darkest joy to ecstatic joy—and they share the lessons learned along the way, reflecting hope for the reader.

If you or someone you know is dealing with grief—caused either by loss of a loved one or by grief caused from regrets or sinful choices in the past—I highly recommend this book. Let the stories minister to you and inspire you. And, at the appropriate time, I encourage you to ask God how He might be calling you to share your story, transparently, as these authors have, to help others.

God uses everything for his purposes—even death and our regrets caused by our own sin. Our healing or forgiveness that He makes possible moves us "from" something to something, just like salvation, when we were saved "from" something "to" something. We are saved from Hell and brought to an eternal life in Haven. We are saved "from" death and regret, and we are saved "to" live out what He brings us "to"—restoration. We are then expected to demonstrate that restoration, by making our forgiveness or healing visible to others. We are forgiven, restored and healed to testify about this transformation in our lives.

The misconception that there is no responsibility after the forgiveness of our sin is pathetically shortsighted and self-centered. Our redemption is a new beginning point that testifies of God's grace. Our restoration allows us to be fruitful and multiply, and to produce good fruit out of bad choices. Redeemed saints of God must be wise in the plan and purpose of man, sin and redemption, as well as marriage and procreation. This concept is not strange and new. This concept is part of new conception called rebirth.

So, let's recap. Let's change a period after we receive forgiveness to a comma, by sharing with others how we came to have an abundant life on Earth and how we are assured to a wondrous eternal life in Heaven. Sharing our testimony will help us make even more spiritual progress, as we trench past our shame.

As we take those steps, we march out of the shadows into His bright light. Then, we become a restored part of God's army once again, and we demonstrate His power to restore. We also show how He has transformed our ashes into beauty through restoration. We also leave what truly needs to be left behind…the guilt of forgiven sin.

31.
The Misconception of Conception: Part 2

Strengthening Strategy:
Living the Christian life in your own wisdom and power…hinders growing up in
Christ.

It has been said that, "Babies are just a lot of noise at one end and a total lack of responsibility at the other." That may be funny, but it is all too real for the parents of a newborn. Babies are absolutely helpless at birth and raising them is very demanding. The parents will never be able to go back to their daily routine and life is about to change more than they had ever imagined.

Perhaps parents should consider leaving their baby in the hospital to be raised? As crazy as that idea sounds, it is more often than not the way we birth people into the family of God.

We touched on this issue a bit in the chapter about wax fruit, but here I want to elaborate on the importance of moving new Christian recruits toward "full maturity." I also want to discuss the incredible responsibility we have once we produce fruit.

Like child-rearing in your own family, raising up "God-men" or disciples in the church must begin immediately after spiritual birth, also known as salvation. It is not the responsibility of church staff to do that, but rather the responsibility of the spiritual parent.

As spiritual parents, we should be committed to be in this maturation process for the long haul. Figuratively speaking, we should care for people from changing diapers to college graduation and leaving the nest. Otherwise, we end up with 25-year-old spiritual babies instead of fully functional, adult single-minded Christian soldiers.

In 1 Corinthians 2:15, Paul gives us a good explanation of the difference between immature Christian babies and spiritual "God-men." He states that mature Christians have wisdom which is different from simple intellect. Now, they can sit in judgment of issues.

Yet Paul says that he cannot be judged by anyone. In verse 16, Paul gives the reason why. It is because his actions are initiated by God and that he is controlled by God's Spirit. You simply cannot argue against that. He had become what God intended for him to be—a mature, Spirit-filled, Spirit-controlled, godly adult.

As we keep reading Paul's letter to the Corinthians in chapter 3, we see that Paul confronts the people with a serious problem that was developing. As much as he would like to address many followers in this group on an adult/spiritual level, he could not. So, Paul addresses the problem by drawing a parallel to something that they can understand and uses a rather "infantile" approach—excuse the pun.

Paul eases them into this confrontation by relating their spiritual growth to the natural growth process of a newborn baby. He tells them that all babies start out the same way—drinking milk and not attempting to eat solid food. He goes on to say that there is nothing wrong with that, because it is perfectly natural (1 Corinthians 3:1–2).

As he continues, Paul doesn't mince words; rather, he plainly states, *"For ye are yet carnal"* (1 Corinthians 3:3, KJV). For the purposes of this discussion, we can use the words unskilled, uneducated or immature to more clearly get the meaning of the word "carnal."

Paul knew these "carnal" people because he had preached to them before when they were first birthed into the family of God. Now, sometime later, he discovers they have not grown in the faith at all. They are "still babies" and Paul is saying that is absolutely **"unnatural,"** in terms of spiritual development.

He continues to explain that, in their infancy, they could not begin to understand spiritual things because they, figuratively speaking, had no teeth to chew with. Nor could they swallow or digest spiritual meat. They could not take in or make use of anything spiritual in the beginning, which is OK...for spiritual babies.

However, Paul did have a problem with these "carnal" people, and it was summed up in one word: "yet." They were still spiritual "babies," but they should have been mature by now.

Our English translation of the Bible fails us a bit here. It uses a Greek word, "carnal" in two places that actually have different meanings. The word "carnal" in 1 Corinthians 3:1–2 is not critical. It means "fleshy material," in other words, "baby skin" which is logical for babies.

But in verse 3, we see that Paul uses a different Greek word for "carnal." (This word choice is critical). He states that they are "yet" carnal. The word "carnal" here means still "flesh-like" after all these years. This word "carnal" states that they are living in the flesh rather than in the spirit. They are still acting like babies and not like mature single-minded Christians.

Paul says he still has to talk baby-talk to them, and therefore, they remain clueless about greater spiritual matters. In addition, they continue to make the mistakes that a spiritual baby would make. The result is that they are still basically useless to further developing the Kingdom of God.

The things they decide to do are done wrong. They choose to do other things at the wrong time, in the wrong way. As a result, all the people in that community are all subject to anyone and everyone's judgment.

Therein lies the second "misconception of conception." Christians were not conceived into the family of God to remain in a spiritually infantile state.

Well, the next step then, since we need to get out of the crib, is to understand what is keeping us in there. So, let's ask ourselves: What keeps us wearing spiritual diapers and feeding on milk? Why aren't we growing spiritual "teeth?"

If we made a list of the reasons why we don't mature spiritually, we would most certainly have to start that list with discipleship. I want to focus not on the list, but on the reason *behind* the list of reasons for a lack of spiritual growth.

The primary reason that many people work harder and accomplish less in the Kingdom of God is because they are working in their own knowledge and strength. Perhaps they haven't been taught effectively by others, or perhaps they just don't listen when they are taught. Either way, as Paul says: *"Your faith should not stand in the wisdom of men, but in the power of God."* (1 Corinthians 2:5, KJV).

To understand more about what happens when people use their own strength rather than relying on God's power, ask yourself this question: Is it possible to go to church, teach, preach, build churches and even send missionaries to foreign lands in the wisdom and strength of man? Sure it is. Is it possible to closely duplicate almost everything that God does or wants to do? Absolutely, but, if it is accomplished solely as a result of man's "fleshy" efforts, it will only create a shadow of what the real work of God could and should be like.

These shadow efforts keep us very busy, which is Satan's preference. We are busy, busy, busy, doing either the wrong thing or doing the right thing, but in our own power and wisdom, in our way. This process is like spinning our wheels; it could produce a lot of smoke and noise, but it doesn't get you anywhere.

If the source of our efforts are not divine in origin, Paul says, we can be *"among,"* or (mixed in with) the spiritually mature, but the things we accomplish are *"doomed to pass away."* (1 Corinthians 2:6, ESV). We may look like spiritually mature people look. We can act like them and even talk like they talk. But if the origin of our efforts is wrong, so is the end result.

Once we are "birthed" or "saved" into the relationship that God intends for man, we must continue the natural progression of attaining a spirit-filled life through growth and *maturity*. If we do not grow, that is unnatural—both in our physical life and in the spiritual life as a Christian.

I have witnessed this problem time and time again in many areas of Christian service. Some people are always busy, but they never seem to get anything done. More often than not, they are so scatter-brained that every part of their lives is in chaos. They engage in much activity, but have nothing to show for it. That's immature, unfocused and double-minded. These futile efforts also prevent us from carrying out our orders that God "conceived" of for each of us to do.

We must not disobey a direct General Order of our Commanding Officer about engaging in lifelong discipleship. If we do, soldiers in our units could fall prey to believing the misconception of conception: that it is OK for them to remain "spiritual infants," and perform no tasks for the Kingdom. Or they could progress to "spiritual toddlerdom" and busy themselves in misguided activity without the power of God's strength. However, such activity could make them overly tired and vulnerable to getting…picked off for good.

Let's make sure, instead, that we obey our General Order. Let's continue training other single-minded Christian soldiers, chiding and pruning them as necessary, so they too have all the tools they need to reproduce and grow…to bear even more fruit.

32.
Dysfunctional Units: It's Not My Job

Strengthening Strategy:
Understanding the difference between being busy and making progress.

You could not possibly know this, but, the "Denoso slap" in the television series NCIS originated with my mom. The TV program copied it, brought it to television and made it famous. But, make no mistake, I was the original crash-test dummy for the head slap.

It started when I was a child growing up in a military family. I learned very quickly that when you are told to do something, you do not ask any questions, you just do it. If you asked, "why," you always got the same response. That's right, the original, one-of-a-kind, "Denoso Slap" to the back of the head. It was usually accompanied by a single-eye-glare that belongs in a "b-rated" or low-budget, horror movie.

The only acceptable response in our family was: "Yes Sir." Then you did whatever you had to do to get the job done—period! Your concerns, interests, plans and opinions were not important or tolerated.

Let me be clear. I don't mean to imply that I could not ask a question. If I did not know how to do a particular task, I was allowed and even encouraged to obtain additional information. But I quickly learned the difference between asking my father a question, and questioning my father. (There was a big difference and much more pain associated with the latter.)

In fact, asking my father a question showed sincere interest in getting the job done correctly. However, questioning my father was seen as an indication that I was interested in a form of bodily injury that made sitting down almost impossible!

These fond memories stayed with me as I grew up and began working for other people. If the boss said to do something, I just did it, no questions. I became the "go-to guy," and I was rewarded for my excellent work ethic.

When I went into business for myself, I expected that same work ethic from my employees, and I led them by example. I was the first to arrive in the morning, and I worked harder than anyone else. At 5 p.m., when everyone headed toward the parking lot, I headed toward the broom, dustpan and rubber gloves.

As a business owner, everything is your business and your responsibility. Good or bad, profit or loss, mop or dust, sink or toilet—it is all yours! Ah, the pride of ownership!

As the boss who sees the greater picture, you have a better perspective of what needs to be done and how it should happen. If you want suggestions, you will ask. Otherwise, you already have the goal clearly defined and comments are not necessary. It is really rather simple: employees do the job they were hired to do, and the paychecks keep coming. What a deal! (In fact, there were many times that I would have gladly swapped jobs with my employees if I could have.)

So let's take a look at a church member's responsibility as if church membership were a business. Pretend that you are the owner. Let's examine a few of the excuses your employees might use when they fail to do their job.

Often when people are asked to teach a Sunday school class, serve in the nursery or do any servant-type task, they get a "deer-in-the-headlight-look" as if to say: *"Who, me? I can't do that!"* Others may not utter a question like that out loud, but their faces implies it.

Another excuse I've heard is *"I don't even have children that age."* Or, they play the classic comparison game and ask, *"What is she going to be doing while I'm doing that?"*

Ever heard this one? *"Isn't that so-and-so's responsibility? Don't we pay them to do that?"*

And here's one that makes me grit my teeth! *"That isn't in my job description."* As a business owner, I only had one job description for my employees—whatever it takes to get the job done. As long as it is not immoral, unethical or illegal—that's your job description, period! Get the job done!

Ladies, here's is an oldie, but a goodie...some church members believe that every woman's ministry was conceived for the expressed purpose of giving the pastor's wife some responsibility. It actually gives her life purpose and validity.

If the pastor's wife has a baby, then it's obvious that she should head up the nursery...Duh!

She gets promoted to teaching the next class just as her own children continue to grow. Once the children are gone, she just keeps teaching older groups until eventually she winds up at the Senior Citizens Center herself eating Jell-O and coloring.

All of these responsibilities are in addition to her standard chores of singing in the choir, decorating the church—and of course—kitchen clean up.

The PKs (Preachers Kids) also have a divine call on their lives. They become responsible for the spiritual well-being of every boy and girl in the church, and PKs must set the standard for all to follow. I think this is where the "zero tolerance" concept actually originated.

Finally, just when you think you have everything worked out and the church is on the right path, it starts to unravel.

It usually starts with someone in the church who has a pet project. That person picks a chairman to organize the project and then the chairman picks a co-chair in case he or she is not there. The co-chair's responsibility is to pick the group leaders. The group leader select team leaders. The team leaders have no workers to do the work because there isn't anyone left...so the project falls apart.

If you were the boss of these employees, I suspect it would not take long for you to start handing out pink slips. Fortunately for me, my church was perfect. (I wanted that to be on the record, just in case any of those in my former church family are reading this.)

As crazy as all that sounds, you may ask, *"Why would anyone ever consider joining a church?"* Well, as bad as that idea may sound based on the excuses that I have just described, I have been a part of churches that weren't like that at all. In fact, I have experienced being part of a fully functional church, and I think that is one of the greatest joys a Christian can have here on Earth.

Nothing compares to a church body full of pumped up, energetic, positive, *mature* thinkers who *expect* to work and *expect* God to perform miracles in their midst. You can't find enough work for them to do and they are always ready to serve.

For instance, my current church requires more than 550 volunteers every week, just to have the basic things run smoothly, like a tightly wound clock—and it usually works quite well. What makes the difference?

Mature Christians make the difference. These Christian Saints know that their service is not about them. Instead, it is all about the Lord and what He wants. *Mature* Christians understand that service is about rising up to meet God's level of expectations in obedience and sacrifice. They bathe service and church needs in prayer, and then they draw on His strength to develop a deeper dedication to do the work.

Your responsibilities are more than just cleaning the church, teaching a class and putting money in the collection plate. These tasks are relatively obvious and generic to every member. They are just the chores—*not the work*. Let me explain what I mean with a brief story…

A young teenage boy from the city made friends with another boy in his class who was from the country. When Fall Break came, the country boy invited the city boy to come home with him to the farm. The city boy eagerly accepted, and he looked forward to learning about farm life.

The first morning at the farm started while it was still dark outside. The city boy was rushed into his clothes and pushed toward the barn with a rake in hand.

The two boys cleaned the barn, fed the chickens and cows, put out hay for the horses and gathered the eggs. Finally, they heard the bell ring signaling that breakfast was ready. They sat down to a huge country breakfast and ate until they could not eat another bite.

The city boy was quite satisfied with their accomplishments, However, his thoughts of fulfillment were quickly dashed when the young farm boy jumped up and said, "Common, we got lots of work to do." The city boy was confused and replied, "Work? What do you think we've been doing?"

The country boy responded, "Oh, those were just the chores...the real work is in the field."

What is the moral of this story? Do not get too involved in the "chores" of the church—serving the members and work that needs to be done inside the church—that you forget to remember that the ultimate goal is the work out in the field.

Church "chores" are good, fun and supportive for the rest of the body. But the chores should prepare us for the work in the field— reaching lost people for Christ, and ultimately, for the harvest when they accept Him. Then, they too, become mature, single-minded Christian soldiers.

Your highest goal should be to find the Lord's specific place for you to serve—both inside and outside the church building. Doing what the Lord designed you to do, using whatever spiritual gift He has given you, is the key to doing whatever you do with excellence and having that work produce good, God-fruit.

If you do not find out exactly where the Lord wants you to work and what he wants you to do, you will be very busy—but ineffective. Misdirected efforts simply turn into futile religious activity. It would be one thing if you just wasted your own time and did not interfere with other members. But people in the wrong place, doing the wrong thing, makes the work of others much harder.

We must also consider the responsibility of every church member to identify, perfect and use their gifts and talents for the church body. That's right, let me repeat that last part...**for the church body**—not for yourself.

The church is not a platform for members to display their wonderful talents and personal interests for their own personal gain. Nor is it just an opportunity for members to share their knowledge, play an instrument or whatever else they enjoy doing. Those activities may play *a part in service* but the emphasis must remain on being active in service *to* and *for* others.

Church service that helps others is where God's children should be applying their gifts so that they are "outstanding in the field"—serving others so that the real, meaningful work will not be...left undone.

33.

Plum Foolish? Or Plum Good?

Strengthening Strategy:
Looking for the quality and quantity that pleases God.

Have you ever thought about the question: Why is it the responsibility of every Christian to ask for forgiveness and be restored?

The reason is that every one of us has a responsibility to be clean so that we can do our part as a single-minded Christian soldier. Part of that training includes allowing God to keep us clean. The Bible tells us that we are vessels of God, and He is not going to put clean things in dirty vessels.

Christians should continually apply the "plum line" of God's Word to their life so that they can see what may not line up. Just in case you don't know, a "plum line" is a string with a weight on it. Carpenters use it to build a wall, using gravity as the unalterable force that will always make the "plum line" straight. Therefore, a "plum line" makes sure that the wall is set straight. Similarly, cultivating a deeper knowledge of God will also help you set you straight, bringing your life in tandem with God's ideal plan and purpose. I'm not sure, but being in line with God and the peace that brings may be where the saying "that's plum good" came from.

That "plum good" relationship enables Him to direct you, empower you and produce fruit through you. In addition, because sin separates us from God, we must constantly and consistently get rid of sin by asking Him for forgiveness and repenting of our sin. Sin prevents us from being clean, and not keeping clean is "plum foolish."

We likely engage in more sinful actions than we can count. We need to ask God to forgive us for all of them. We could list them all, but they all boil down to two basic categories that we need to discuss. It will help us know the two primary pitfalls to help us stay on mission as single-minded Christian soldiers.

First, we commit **sins of commission, which are those that we choose to commit**. See the word, "commit" in the word "commission?" So what's an example of a sin of commission? If you were to tell an untruth to someone, you have willfully lied to them. You have committed the sin of lying.

The second type of sins are just as harmful because we **did not do something we should have done**. Those are called **sins of "omission."** We have "omitted" doing what was right. For example: Jesus says that we are to forgive others just as God forgave us. You can't "omit" forgiveness and maintain a correct relationship with the One who first forgave you.

Sin must be rooted out as often as necessary, sometimes as often as several times a day, because it hinders our fellowship with God and others. Sin separates us from God and tears down the lines of communication with Him. God cannot, and will not, allow unclean people to do holy things. So stay clean and useful by implementing some basic steps on a regular basis.

One of those steps is to constantly ask God to reveal hidden sins to us. Then ask for forgiveness for those sins. We are very aware of some of our sins, but some are there that we did not realize. Or, we may have unconfessed sins that we have just forgotten about. Forgiveness is another step that cleanses and restores our relationship with God, and we need that restoration for routine Christian maintenance! Engaging in the steps I have just described for restoration is your personal responsibility to God, yourself *and* others.

Forgiveness is an important key to maintaining the right relationship with God. It is our own personal forgiveness that gives us the authority to share our testimony with others so they too can be forgiven.

Unfortunately, many people might not share their testimony because they feel that the responsibility for adding more believers is only the pastor's job. Well, this may come as a surprise to you, but it's not the pastor's responsibility to do that work. *The pastor's job is to teach and equip each church member to do the work of sharing their faith—and one aspect of that work is sharing a testimony.*

The pastor's duty, with his messages, example and interactions with you, is to provide a Holy yardstick to show you whether or not you measure up to your call. He is to supply a magnifying glass that will reveal your flaws and use the Bible as a "plum line" to determine if your walk is straight or not.

Think about that for just a minute…a plum line cannot make a crooked wall straight. It can only tell you if the wall is crooked. The pastor cannot straighten you out either. He can only let you know if you are crooked according to the spiritual plum line—the Bible. The bottom line is that it is your responsibility to get straight and stay straight.

I guess I could have written this book in reverse and made it a whole lot shorter. This would be the only chapter and just one sentence in the chapter would read: "Get your own spiritual life right, and everything else will be all right." Amen, have a good day…the end. (And the cost of the book would be two cents.)

For church members to become good single-minded Christian soldiers, they must obey orders, find their place of service, maintain a Godly life and keep developing a close relationship to God. We must also do our jobs well and train others to do the same. Our missions must be done through sacrifice, dedication and prayer. I promise you, if you do these things, you will avoid being "plum foolish." Instead, the fruit you produce will be . . ."plum good!"

34.
Spiritual Multitasking

Strengthening Strategy:
Understanding our problems—we don't know...what we don't know.

Everything in our world is already traveling at lightning speed. In fact, it seems to be increasing in velocity every day. As our own little sphere of influence increases in speed, the demand to take on additional responsibilities increases at the same rate. And, we must try to do everything in the same 24-hour-period that we had yesterday. Time is the only thing that is *not* increasing. So, those who master the art of multitasking will have a definite edge.

Although multitasking allows you to work on several things at one time, it also divides your focus and energy. Therefore, people who can multitask must also be able to prioritize and sort through objectives to achieve the ultimate goal without the workload increasing exponentially.

If our brains could only continue to increase in ability to meet the growing demands—then we wouldn't have a problem. But they don't. Actually, the opposite is true: as the demand for speed increases, our bodies and minds abilities are actually decreasing. We are not really designed to keep up.

Some things of lesser importance must be set aside to make time for these new priorities. Let's face it, the older we get, the less inclined we are to change anything, and increasing the workload is simply not an option. We don't do anything fast any more—except fall asleep.

Multitasking and organization sounds good on the surface, but those processes demand much attention. The tendency is to succumb to the pressures of life to the point that we cannot take time to dream. If we do not dream, we can only make decisions based on what we already know to be reality. And, we will never know what might have been if we only dreamed it.

My Dad said many things that I think I'm just now beginning to understand. Like, *"Son, just hush. When you are talking, you can only talk about what you already know. When you listen, you learn some things you don't know or you may realize what's wrong with what you thought you did know."*

That's not to say that our lives should be stationary either. As we grow, more growing needs to take place. So, we need balance. The Bible is filled with examples of God constantly moving, doing, creating, remaking, etc. We are created in His image and we must be continually moving and growing as well. We have one problem that God does not have, though—we have more and more to do, but we have less and less time.

Therefore, we must also become proficient at multitasking in the Christian life. Our tasks may call for changing or modifying priorities. Focusing our energies and efforts can achieve new goals or enable us to pursue new directions.

Lee Iacocca is the man that saved Chrysler Motors in 1979 from bankruptcy and made them profitable again for more than 25 years. Then the government jumped in after the economy crashed in 2008, but's that's another story. Anyway, Lee adopted a slogan that totally described his game plan in just a few short words; *"Lead, follow or get out of the way!"*

That was a great marketing tool for selling Chryslers. But, don't be too eager to adopt every catchy slogan or marketing strategy that the world comes up with or try to apply those items too quickly to supernatural matters. Our slogan should be more like…"He leads, I follow and try to stay out of HIS way."

Many of us are under so much pressure, and we are so focused on the worldly demands of life that our spiritual lives suffers. If we are not careful, our walk with God will slow to a snail's pace and our focus will become so distorted that we become useless to the Kingdom.

Some congregations that previously provided a routine concoction of Sunday morning, Sunday night and Wednesday night services have had to make some radical changes. They have turned their programs and events into a multitasking, fast-paced cornucopia. They include everything from social outings and meals to celebrations and multi-media entertainment extravaganzas!

Some mega-churches have enough programs to keep even the most energetic family running from one thing to another—every day, all week long.

I'm not saying change is bad. We should all be looking for ways to improve our personal Christian lives and prioritize our efforts. The improvement could be worthwhile as long as it is in line with the Gospel message and does not compromise it. The key question to ask yourself amidst many choices is: Does this endeavor produce fruit? If it does, prioritize it. If it doesn't, get rid of it and find one that does.

So, no matter how much you already know or have learned, you must still make room for what you don't know: both in this world and in the spiritual one. One person has said, *"The problem with not knowing is that you don't even know, what you don't know."*

When I mentioned that we needed time to dream, I did not mean day-dreaming. The dreaming I am speaking of is defined in the dictionary as: *"An idea or vision that is created in your imagination and that is not real."* Another dictionary says to dream is: *"To conceive as possible."* I like both definitions. One speaks of things that are not real—yet! The other says to me...why not?

Depending on which translation you use, the Bible lists about 30 examples of dreams playing a major role in finding God's will and changing the world. Two of my favorite dreams in Scripture include Joseph's dream in Genesis (37:8, KJV), when God revealed to Joseph that he would reign over his older brothers, and in Ephesians (3:20, KJV), when God tells us that He is able to do more than we ever desired, thought of, hoped for or *dreamed* of.

Dreams are not to be considered just nice thoughts or fantasies. God made us have dreams to get us to think outside the human box of understanding so that we could *ponder* the possibilities.

When the angel Gabriel explained all that would happen to Mary, the mother of Jesus, the Scripture says, *"…She kept revolving in her mind"* (Luke 1:29, AMPC). That kind of "revolving" is the word we would use, to say that she "pondered" what the angel had said.

That kind of pondering is not day-dreaming—it is using spiritual discernment. Seeing with the mind's eye clarifies things that make sense. In Mary's case, however, it also helped her process things in her heart that were beyond what she could see and naturally comprehend in her mind.

How else could she have comprehended the thought of having a child without knowing a man? It didn't make sense. It wasn't logical. It had never happened before. All that she knew to be true in her intellect and common sense told her that this story was not possible.

I am not sure if Mary ever came to know all the spiritual details of her having a son without knowing a man. Maybe she did, or maybe she didn't, but that's not the point. The point is that she *pondered* those things in her **heart**—not her head! She set aside time to consider, think and then, go deeper. I like to think that she "heart-pondered" them.

How does Mary's pondering apply to our discussion of today's multitasking? Because I think that our spiritual "multitasking" must include pondering (contemplating) and dreaming (envisioning what is not yet real). It must also include discerning what thoughts are spiritual reasoning and what thoughts are just wishes or desires.

But in all of this spiritual multitasking, our ultimate goal must maintain its priority. Our vision must be clear and our efforts must not be swayed. We must stay focused and remove distractions. The Gospel cannot—and must not—be compromised. What is our ultimate goal? Paul said it like this, *"For me to live, is Christ. To die is gain"* (Philippians 1:21, KJV). So, our goal is to live the Gospel, teach the Gospel and maintain the integrity of the Gospel for those that follow after us.

We are to live a life patterned after the life of God's Son and after that, life on earth really gets good!

Even when we are mature in our walk with Christ and experiencing fulfillment and His supernatural blessings, we must keep the main thing, the main thing. In other words, we must stay connected to Him to keep growing deeper and deeper with Him. For me, there is no option, and there is no second-best and there is…no fall-back position.

35.

PC Terrorism

Strengthening Strategy:
Being authentic, recognizing the truth and defending the faith.

Just when you think you are on the right track, in comes "political correctness" again! "Political correctness" wants close or average to be good enough for everything. "Politically correct" proponents want everyone to be a winner so that no one's psyche gets bumped. Well, brace yourself people, because God is in the Holy psyche bumpin' business!

This kind of "politically correct" brain cancer drives me nuts! The intellectual short-comer that came up with this catch-all phrase is terrorizing everyone and trying to disrupt everything. The severity of this reality became clear to me when my grandson was playing Little League baseball. Since he was my favorite grandson, I naturally volunteered to sponsor his team.

Sponsoring is actually an all-inclusive marketing term that means you pay for a bunch of stuff, but we didn't care! Nana and Papa were totally on board with that. Besides, we felt blessed to help launch the career of a future Major League World Series MVP.

When it came to making the trophy selections, I was determined to make this year super. The trophies had to be big and they had to be special. Not some goofy used baseball super-glued on a piece of Plexiglas. No sir—not from this sponsor! I'm talking big, shiny hummers with some substance to them! I didn't care if they had to have training wheels and you had to pull them with a truck.

So I was thinking…three, maybe four, really nice trophies. Perhaps we would have awards for first place, most home runs, best batting average, sportsmanship and of course…a sponsor's trophy. Well, I was about to get a rather rude awakening!

This boy's Walmart wallet was fixing to be introduced to the Sax 5th Avenue reality of what it means to be a sponsor in this "politically correct" day and age. It was not just one team championship trophy, everyone on the team had to get their own championship trophy as well. That's 26 championship trophies. Hold up though…I'm still not finished!

Next were the second place, third place and fourth place awards. Remember, these are not just team trophies, but *each person* on the second place, third place team got their own trophy in addition to the team trophy. Hang on…I'm still not done.

The shock is setting in and I am going in and out of consciousness so everything from that point on is a bit sketchy. I think there was also honorable mention, most improved, high attendance, best sportsmanship, highest batting average, coaches trophies, coach of the year, the bat-boy and even the mascot got one. I think it was a big brass Milk Bone—I was glad their mascot wasn't a whale.

Oh yeah, I got something for being the sponsor…a nice keychain.

Hold on…we're still not done. If the team would have made District Champs, we would start that trophy process all over again. If they would have gone to the State Championship and the Little League World Series, I would have had to sell my house to pay the trophy bill! I was never so happy to see a team lose. I was probably the only one in the bleachers cheering. *"Whoopee, we lost! Let's hear it for the losers!"*

When the ceremony was over, even the kids that were not the champs had trouble carrying all their trophies to the car. It looked like a giant garage sale at a chrome factory!

In today's culture of everyone being labeled a winner, it can be difficult to know who the true winners and losers are. But, in life, it seems the winners that rise to the top are those who are the most authentic, focused and single-minded toward a goal.

So, in this "politically correctness" on steroids world, how do we ascertain authenticity—and how do we develop it in greater measure in ourselves? We examine the evidence closely to see if we are on track as single-minded soldiers who are authentically living for Christ. To test ourselves, we could ask the following questions: Does Christ-like character shine through every facet of our lives? Do we live up to God's standard more often than not? Do we admit our shortcomings when we fail? Do we ask God and others for forgiveness whenever necessary? Do we diligently seek to grow in Christ each day?

If we can answer these questions affirmatively—being completely honest—He will help us become a true representative for God, our Commander. People will know that we, as single-minded Christian soldiers, belong to Him. They will want to know Him because of the light they see in us and they will not want...to be left out.

36. Be All You Are

Strengthening Strategy:
Committing to standing tall, being bulletproof and believing that failure is not an
option!

Well, here we are at the end of our journey. Our message is one of preparation and implementation. The Christian goal is to "be" what we "are," and to live out what we claim to be, which is God's example of Grace to others. The Bible refers to this goal as the "High Calling" and did you notice, nowhere does it ever say: "…and the runner up is…"

The United States Army has a great slogan that I wish Christians had thought of first. It is: "Be all you can be." We need to change it up a just a bit and say, "Be all that you actually are." That, dear Saint of God, is our single-minded Christian soldier goal. Be the winner that we are, in Christ. Be Christ-like in everything—and don't settle for second best.

To be the winner that we claim to be, we must totally commit to the end. There is no rising to a plateau and coasting. We must always be moving upward and forward. There is no grading on a curve.

For the single-minded military soldier, failure on the battlefield is not an option. And so it should be for the single-minded Christian soldier. Our lifelong goal should be: living a Christ-like, Spirit-filled life to the fullest with failure not being an option. After all, we operate in the strength of God Himself.

Christian multitasking is double work. We must multitask both in the physical world and the spiritual realm. For instance, I am a son of my parents, a husband to my wife, a father to my children, an owner of a business and a boss to my employees. That's multitasking!

In addition, in the spiritual multitasking realm, I am a son of the Heavenly Father, I am a Bride to His Son, I am His disciple, I am one of His children, I am a worker in church and I am a witness to everyone whom I come into contact with. How's that for a full plate?

To be a Christ-like single-minded soldier also involves dreaming. It involves dreaming that stretches the spiritual mind and enlarges concepts and the ability to discern. I must have discernment about what I think I know and what I have yet to discover.

As I grow and learn more about my Heavenly Father, my responsibility and my goal does not change—it is singularly focused on becoming more Christ-like. But as the issues, challenges, disappointments and frustrations come each day, I am required to spiritually multitask, refocus, prioritize and dream. I am constantly in the practice of teaching my mind, controlling my emotions, directing my will and keeping the goal ever fixed. I will never let myself compromise who I am in Christ.

Like the single-minded soldier on the battlefield, I may have to change my tactics, improve my weaponry and do more multitasking as I ponder the plan of attack. But rest assured, I know my orders. I will always be moving forward and up the hill.

I must always declare: *"I am a winner because I serve a victor. Christ is victory!"* For me, there is no second place, no runner up or no honorable mention. *There can be no shadows*—only Christ.

As we press toward the mark of the high calling on our lives to live for Christ, we should look forward to receiving our crown—not a trophy. We should long to hear the words: "Welcome home, you good and faithful, multitasking, discerning and pondering dreamer and worker…enter in." And, like every good single-minded Christian soldier, let us be determined never to…leave anyone behind.

I would like to leave you with the only poem I have ever written. I'm including it because running well is required to be an authentic single-minded soldier, and I pray it will encourage you just a bit more. **Will you join me in the race?**

Why Run?

If God expects me to be like his Son
In this race of New Life I've just begun,
How am I to compete with the one
Who already ran the race and won?

Where does the desire to win retreat
When the certainty of the race is defeat?
I cannot possibly accomplish the feat…
that Jesus did, I am left to retreat.

To avoid the dismay of a race not won,
Would I be better off not to have run?
I could never be anywhere close to the Son,
Yes, perhaps better, if I'd never begun.

Even though the time and effort I did not spend,
because I knew I could not endure to the end.
Rather, I'll sit on the sideline and wait till the end
in hopes that a victor's welcome…I still can attend.

Such a lofty thought to dream of the gold or
even consider such a thought is just too bold.
It's not that my heart has grown cold,
but for this type of race, I'm just too old.

Then I realize it is not important where I finish
and the excitement of the race need not diminish.
I feel the power and desire replenish as
I remember my concern should be…to finish.

So run and run fast till the race is done
for it is with Him and not against Him I run.
Striving to please him and become like the Son,

You see…the faithful who run, have already won!

Though not yet in Heaven to take my place
among all the others who have finished the race.
The pleasure I see on my Father's face,
encourages me not just to run, but pick up the pace!

For I realized now what was too hard to see…
He runs the race, it is not me.

Bruce A. Peltier

Acknowledgments

I believe that any honest author will concede—to some degree—that a professional editor for any work is absolutely indispensable. Therefore, sharing the credit for its success is an obvious necessity. Thank you to my editor, Loral Robben Pepoon, who helped me to clarify content and sculpt my writing to make it more in line with other published material out there. You can find out about Loral and her various editorial services at Cowriterpro.com.

Thank you to my publisher, Selah Press, who spearheaded the cover design and the formatting of this book in print and ebook form. I am very grateful for your expertise and technical know-how. Learn more about Selah Press at Selah-press.com.

I also owe thanks to family members and friends who encouraged me to keep going on this journey of writing to make the publishing of this book come to fruition. I would like to especially thank those who read sections of this book and gave me input on the content.

About the Author

Early life. I started life as the son of a career military officer, living in many countries in Europe, Japan and Southeast Asia—as well as many parts of the good ol' USA.

Education. I am only a high school graduate with one year of college coursework. I was majoring in marketing when I stopped taking classes formally, but I feel like I have a Ph.D. in street-smarts with two areas of specialty: one in confidence and one in humor, with two minors, one in listening and one in modesty.

Military Service. I spent three years in the Army and was Honorably Discharged. I served two tours in Vietnam flying around in helicopters sitting behind a machine gun. I was awarded 33 Air Medals and the Purple Heart for wounds received in action.

Professional Life. I have been a dishwasher, short-order cook, K-Mart clerk, clothing salesman, debt collector and jet aircraft assembly lineman. I have been self-employed for most of my income-producing career as an Aviation Insurance Specialist. I currently own and run two businesses that I started more than 25 years ago.

One is an Aviation Insurance Specialty Company that insures all types of Aviation related risks internationally.
Alliance International Marketing, LLC
www.goodaiminternational.com

The other is an Emergency Transportation Expense Reimbursement Program (a supplement to Major Medical Insurance Policy) that I designed, wrote and successfully marketed to a Fortune 500 company, ***FIRSTrate, Inc.***, of Columbia, Tennessee.

Ministry. During the time that I have owned and operated these two businesses, I was also a Sunday school teacher for more than 35 years, a reserve deputy sheriff for seven years and a pastor.

Ongoing Hobby. Oh yes, I have also been a beginner at golf for more than 35 years.

About My Family. I have been married for 43 years to my one and only wife, Kaye. She has served churches for more than 50 years as a minister of music, a music and vocal teacher and coach as well as church pianist and organist. In her spare time, she is a full-time mother, business partner and best friend.

Kaye is also a licensed music practitioner; she uses music for healing purposes and helps those who are transitioning from this life. She is also a published author. Her first children's book is accompanied by a song she wrote, all based on scripture dealing with "The Fruit of the Spirit."

Kaye and I have one daughter, Kayce, who is married to Trevor. They have one child, our grandson, Tanner.

My future. I still struggle with what I will do for a living when I grow up.

Live your life in such a way
that those who know you
But do not know God,
Will come to know God
because they know you.

Dad at age 19. Just got his wings!

My Dad, left, Lieutenant Colonel Reginald A. Peltier, who served in World War II, in the Korean War and twice in Vietnam; and me, right, Specialist, 5th Class Bruce A. Peltier, who served twice in Vietnam. This photo was taken on Veterans Day, 1991, the year before Dad went home to meet the Lord, in 1992.

My brother, Gene A. Peltier, was deployed five times in the span of more than 30 years. In the early 1960s, he served in Germany for three years. In 1982, he was stationed in the Middle East in Lebanon. In the early 1990s, he served in Saudi Arabia in the First Gulf War, as well as in Pakistan and Korea.

Other Single-Minded Peltier's, my four nephews, who are currently serving or who have served...Left to right, Sargent First Class Gene

Peltier, Jr. (Tony), stationed in San Antonio, Texas; Sargent Christopher Peltier, who has been stationed on four U.S. bases and one in Korea; Staff Sargent Bruce Peltier, who was deployed four times in Iraq and Afghanistan between 2003 and 2012; and Staff Sargent Brad-Lee Peltier, who was deployed in Iraq and Afghanistan three times between 2006 and 2011.

www.ingramcontent.com/pod-product-compliance
Lightning Source LLC
Chambersburg PA
CBHW061143040426
42445CB00013B/1529